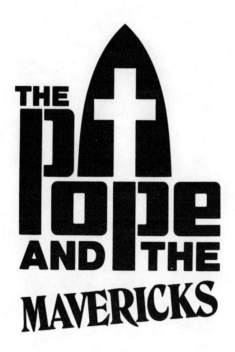

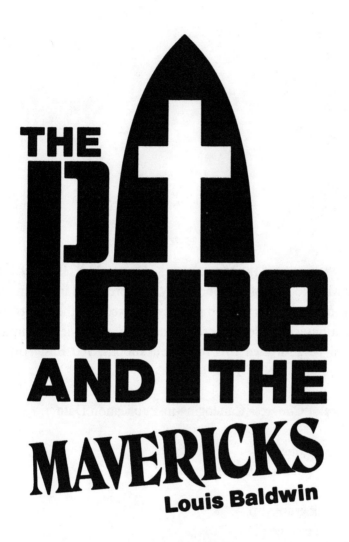

THE POPE AND THE MAVERICKS

Louis Baldwin

PROMETHEUS BOOKS
Buffalo, New York

Library of Congress Cataloging-in-Publication Data

Baldwin, Louis.
    The Pope and the mavericks.

    Bibliography: p.
    Includes index.
    1. Catholic Church—Controversial literature.
2. Dissenters, Religious. 3. Popes—Infallibility.
4. John Paul II, Pope, 1920–   . Papacy—History.
I. Title.
BX 1779.5.B35   1988   282   88-15103
ISBN 0-87975-466-4

To Ginnie, with love

Contents

Foreword   *9*

John Paul II   *11*
    The Writer   *12*
    The Pole   *13*
    The Authoritarian   *14*
Hans Küng   *23*
Edward Schillebeeckx   *49*
Charles E. Curran   *63*
The Liberation Theologians   *81*
    Gustavo Gutiérrez   *82*
    Leonardo Boff   *89*
Raymond Hunthausen   *97*
Joseph Ratzinger   *105*

A Papal Tradition   *115*
    John XII (955–63)   *116*
    Benedict IX (1032–46)   *120*

CONTENTS

Boniface VIII (1294–1303)   *123*
Urban VI (1378–89)   *128*
Alexander VI 1492–1503)   *130*
Leo X (1513–21)   *134*
Clement VII (1523–34)   *136*
Pius IX (1846–78)   *142*
Leo XIII (1878–1903)   *146*
Pius X (1903–14)   *147*
Benedict XV (1914–22)   *151*
Pius XI (1922–39)   *153*
Pius XII (1939–58)   *156*
John XXIII (1958–63)   *159*
Paul VI (1963–78)   *160*
Other Popes, Other Mavericks   *167*
Urban VIII and Galileo (1564–1642)   *168*
Innocent XI and Richard Simon (1638–1712)   *173*
Innocent XII and François Fénelon (1651–1715)   *175*
Gregory XVI and Felicité de Lamennais (1782–1854)   *178*
Pius IX and Antonio Rosmini-Serbati (1797–1855)   *182*
Pius X and Alfred Loisy (1857–1940)   *185*
Pius XI and Pierre Teilhard de Chardin (1881–1955)   *189*
Pius XII and John Courtney Murray (1904–67)   *192*

Afterword   *199*

Bibliography   *205*

Index   *215*

Foreword

During the televised tedium of 1987's Congressional Iranscam hearings one of the few moments of entertainment came when a witness described a Marine officer standing at attention while talking on the telephone with the president. If *that* is possible, then there may well be Catholics who kneel whenever the pope appears on television.

This book is not for them, nor for anyone else, Catholic or otherwise, with similar inclinations. But if you are curious about, or troubled by, the promotion of intellectual tyranny under John Paul & Co., if you are acquainted but not familar with the heterodox views proscribed by Rome but held by many if not most Catholics, and if you would like a brief account of such views—as well as of the people who have advanced them, and especially of the authority by which Rome silences such dissent—the following pages may provide some food for conscientious thought.

John Paul II

Of the present pope it has been said that there are many John Pauls—priest, bishop, theologian, philosopher, poet, actor, linguist, skier, hiker, swimmer, and so on. Karol Wojtyla, a.k.a. John Paul II, is a man of parts, in several ways.

As pope and public figure, he surely exists very much in the eye of each beholder. The bead-telling, candle-lighting, forelock-pulling, very Roman Catholic can envision His Holiness, a celebrity of impeccable sanctity and divinely inspired wisdom whose opinions on matters of faith and morals are part of God's unquestionable law. At the other end of the spectrum the cheek-tonguing, head-shaking, eye-narrowing, not so Roman Catholic can espy an emperor without so many clothes whose delusions of authoritarian grandeur perpetuate the intellectual, or anti-intellectual, tyranny for which Rome has so long been famous.

When the real John Paul stands up, he of course appears somewhere in between, sometimes near this end, sometimes near that, depending on how close he then happens to be to the bottom line. If we peer at him through the mythology created by adoring biographers and public-relations advisers, we seem to glimpse a person of substance: not only affably personable but also intelligent, conscientious, thoughtful (in both senses), courageous, forgiving, dedicated. Although he told one interviewer that he had never had a mystical experience, he is clearly a mystic in good standing, devoted to symbolism for things unseen and, indeed, often for things unknown. He is a published poet and philosopher, but, like Teilhard, he is much more poet than philosopher.

THE WRITER

As a philosopher he tried to reconcile Christianity and humanism, that bugaboo of religious fundamentalists, by stressing the value of the human being made in the image of God; his approach, based on Catholic dogma, doubtless meant more to some Christians than to humanists. As a moralist he mined the same vein in lectures at the Catholic University in Lublin, Poland (published in book form as *Love and Responsibility*), stressing the importance of the human person in erotic love and of selfless love in that relationship; here again his approach doubtless restricted his work's appeal to the pious (of whom there are plenty in Poland). His philosophical and theological work generally consists of unsupported assertions weaving elaborate, mystical tapestries with threads drawn from the Bible and the Roman catechism. (One frustrated reviewer commented that Wojtyla doesn't present arguments, he makes pronouncements.) The poetic, abstract, mystical character of his prose evidently raises some like-minded readers to a pitch of ecstasy while lowering others into a slough of puzzled despond. (Another scholarly critic, perhaps more candid than most, remarked that he had read Wojtyla's *The Acting Person* twice without being sure that he understood it.)

His poetry is at least as mystical, as well as being more personal, subjective, contemplative and introspective. It sometimes offers striking metaphors, as in "the dark of trampled stars," and sometimes great compression of thought, as in "that amazement which will become the essence of eternity." Probably its messages shine out more clearly in the Polish language, and in the Polish milieu.

THE POLE

That Polish milieu may explain a great deal about his attitudes. The Poles have suffered enough from the Russians, during a history of hostility but especially in the current climate of oppression, to account for the patriotic Wojtyla's tough anti-Communism, which resembles that of the first-term Ronald Reagan. Beyond the Soviet ingredient, this is *atheistic* Communism, leading Cardinal Wojtyla to say, in a speech in Manhattan in 1976, "We are now facing the final confrontation between the Church and the anti-Church, of the Gospel versus the anti-Gospel . . . It is not only a trial of our nation and the Church, but in a sense a test of 2000 years of culture and Christian civilization. . . ."

But he is not only a Pole, he is a Polish Catholic. Even today the country is 95% Roman Catholic, and more intensely so than elsewhere because the people have been forced by political adversity to look to the church for protection, moral support, and consolation. The intensity doubtless explains the conspicuously emotional strain in Polish Catholicism, expressed in such things as widespread church attendance defying state opposition, sentimental attachment to this church or that parish, ardent devotion to this or that saint (especially St. Stanislaus, the national patron), fond subservience to hierarchy and clergy, and a general attitude and behavior that, say, a Vatican prelate would consider highly commendable in the Church Militant. It may also explain Karol Wojtyla's single-minded emphasis on "the truth" as well as his deep affection for Our Lady. He has defined freedom, for instance, as knowing "the true good" and then choosing it; and, unlike the dying John XXIII's "Jesu!," his near-death exclamation (after the assassination attempt) was "Madonna!"

THE AUTHORITARIAN

The "truth" to which he is dedicated is essentially that of the catechism. On the indispensable virtue of faith, for example, he told an interviewer, "Personally, I would not discount the old catechism which I learned in primary school: faith is 'to admit as truth what God has revealed and what the Church gives us to believe.' " For "the Church," of course, read "Rome." Despite all the recent, postconciliar talk about "the people of God" and "the priesthood of the laity," the sole focus of "the truth" is Rome. And today that means John Paul II & Co.

The particular "company" in this case is that branch of the Roman Curia which has come to be known, among admirers and critics, as the CDF, or the Congregation for the Doctrine of the Faith, formerly the Holy Office and, still earlier, the Inquisition. This sort of genealogy is common in the Vatican, where great pride is taken in a past which, in a less self-congratulatory environment, would be a source of acute embarrassment. (Vatican II conceded that the Church "is by no means unaware that down through the centuries there have been among her members, both clerical and lay, some who were disloyal to the Spirit of God"; "papal" and "episcopal" should have been included, but that would be expecting too much.) Amid all the medieval, *Mikado*-worthy monikers like "Your Holiness" and "Your Eminence," it is hardly surprising that corporate narcissism has become both chronic and endemic "down through the centuries." Or that the CDF has developed an overpowering taste for the kind of universal intellectual groveling that it calls "internal assent."

Thus when Paul VI, abetted by the CDF, issued his notorious encyclical *Humanae Vitae* flatly condemning all "artificial" birth control, after a commission which he had appointed recommended a gentler approach, he did so simply on the grounds that this was what Rome had taught in the past. In that same past Rome has taught also that charging interest was morally wrong, that the idea of a central sun in the solar system was too dangerous to be held openly, that pleasure in marital sex was sinful, that non-Catholics could never make it to heaven, that religious freedom was an abomination—and so on. The past tense suggests how firmly these opinions are held today. We have all met the kind of person who adamantly insists that he has *not* changed his mind.

And we might diagnose such a person as suffering from

chronic deduction. That is, he deduces conclusions from general principles, as some of us may remember from Philosophy 101. For instance, his general principle in this case could be that he's always right, in which case he must have been right in saying yesterday that circles are square and today that circles are triangular. In contrast, the inductive thinker would examine a representative sample of circles, squares and triangles, and perhaps his deductive friend's mental stability.

Rome is somewhat similarly in the grip of deduction. (Sherlock Holmes, incidentally, engaged much more in induction than deduction.) The basic Vatican syllogism might read, "All our opinions are protected from error by the Holy Spirit; this is one of our opinions; therefore it is protected from error." Since the logic is valid, if the major premise is "the truth," then so is the conclusion, and if anyone cares to question it, let him be anathema. But also because the logic is valid, any real-world contradiction between one opinion and another denies the premise, and the historical record offers enough contradictions for Vatican prelates acquainted with induction to decide that maybe Gospel metaphors like "the keys of the kingdom" and "feed my sheep" don't absolutely guarantee that *all* the opinions are infallible. And so the syllogism became "Some of our opinions are protected from error by the Holy Spirit; this is one of our opinions; therefore, er, it is protected from error."

So much for the validity of the syllogism. Its deterioration has led to phrases like "ex cathedra," which essentially means that an opinion is infallible only if it is declared to be infallible by the infallible person (or group) issuing it. This in turn has led to a great reluctance to issue officially infallible statements.

Since Pius IX infallibly declared himself (and his predecessors and successors) infallible in 1870, only one such statement has been offered to the salivating faithful. In 1950 Pius XII announced that the Virgin Mary had been taken bodily into heaven; this is a comfortably mystical assertion, safe from contradiction because there is not a shred of inductive evidence available for or against it. Not that such evidence would make much difference: as John Paul has said, the chief mission of Catholic pastors, from pope to curate, "is to be teachers of the truth—not a human rational truth, but the truth which comes from God."

The term "ex cathedra" stayed on the Vatican flagpole for a number of years, but the ecclesiastical saluting was never much more than half-hearted. It has been replaced today by "magisterium," a favorite of John Paul's, referring to the general teaching authority of the Church, which is more or less infallible depending on the importance of the subject. "More or less," in the Roman view, means much more more than less, needless to add. The hoary maxim, *Roma locuta, causa finita* ("Rome having spoken, the case is closed"), is still alive and well and living in the Vatican. John Paul, in his first speech as pope, spoke of the need for "unwavering obedience to the Magisterium of Peter," and soon thereafter announced his "deepest hopes" for a "renewed emphasis on sound doctrine and discipline in the life of the Church."

Rome's commitment to deduction also leads to flights of fancy drawn from "the truth" without reference to the real world. They are regularly presented as true of all cases, although they clearly may be true only of some. Thus John Paul, from the premise that all artificial abortion is murder, somehow deduced that it destroys the family—it must, because murder is immoral, and anything immoral destroys the family—adding that it does so because the existing children in the family will know about it and feel threatened! It is equally clear that "to attack unborn life at any moment from its conception is to undermine the whole moral order which is the true guardian of the well-being of man."

Further, since all artificial contraception is immoral, it follows that a couple resorting to it will "ruin the spontaneity and depth of their relationship," as though such qualities of the relationship will be strengthened by anxiety over the problems arising out of uninhibited procreation. ("Intercourse is necessary to love," he has said elsewhere, "not just to procreation.") To those who might question the reliability of professional celibates' pontificating on the intimate psychology of married life, he offers the standard riposte that the "lack of direct personal experience is no handicap because they possess a great deal of experience at second hand, derived from their pastoral work," as though the people who come to them for confession and/or counseling constitute a random, representative sample of married couples. Another dictum presumably follows also, that "sexual morality as everyone knows is a universal phenomenon, something common to all humanity."

Such absolutes, such universals seem to characterize his mental furniture. His attitude toward clerical celibacy could hardly be more rigid if that requirement were carved in the stone of the Ten Commandments: you've made your bed, now lie in it—alone.

To seminarians in Philadelphia in 1979 he offered this formi-

dable encouragement: "Human dignity requires that you maintain this commitment, that you keep your promise to Christ
no matter what difficulties you may encounter and no matter
what temptations you may be exposed to." Note that human
dignity, not Rome, requires adherence to the vow of celibacy,
since a virtually infallible magisterium must be consonant with,
if not the source of, human dignity—which Rome may nevertheless overrule at any time by lifting the requirement. That year
he also inspired American nuns: "Your life must be characterized
by a complete availability, a readiness to serve as the needs
of the Church require." And he couldn't resist adding a comment
on a vital subject that seems continually to gnaw at his Polish
Catholic sensibilities: "It is not unimportant that your
consecration to God should be manifested in the permanent
exterior sign of a simple and suitable religious garb." Back to
the all-enveloping shrouds, ladies.

His persistent attention to externals like this doubtless fits
in well with his and his present colleagues' conspicuous, professional preoccupation with the saying of "Lord, Lord" (Mt 7:21).
Indeed, it may have something to do with his early opinion
on the need for paragons as paradigms: in his doctoral thesis
on Catholicism and phenomenology he stressed the importance
of "models" in moral development, and what more splendid
models could there be than cardinals singing hymns?

Such public piety and supreme self-assurance as Rome dis-
plays can be ascribed to a genuine conviction on the part of
John Paul & Co. that they have a divinely ordained duty to
tell the sheep what to think and do. When we recognize that
they (or at least most of them, surely) firmly believe that they

will be held individually accountable at the Last Judgment for their performance of this duty, we may begin to understand how they can be so rigid, so dependent on tradition for a feeling of security. For they cannot know whether they will be dealing with a merciful Jesus on Judgment Day or perhaps with the stern, genocidal God of the Book of Joshua, compared with whom dissidents and mavericks are inconsequential problems indeed.

Against all this one might cite a remark of Cardinal Wojtyla's quoted in *Osservatore Romano* in 1976: "One can understand that a man may search and not find; one can understand that he may deny; but it is incomprehensible that a man should be told: 'You may not believe.'" At the time he must have been thinking of those despots on the other side of the Iron Curtain. On this side he was concerned about "liberal regimes, where men are sick with affluence and an overdose of freedom."

*　　*　　*

Karol Wojtyla (sounds like Woyteena) was born in May 1920 in Wadowice, a small town southeast of Cracow. As a student of literature at Jagiellonian University in Cracow after 1938, he joined literary-discussion and theatrical groups. After the Nazis invaded and occupied his country, he worked as a laborer in a quarry and in a chemical factory, in war-essential jobs that kept him out of the draft, and in his spare time continued with poetry readings and theater activities (now clandestine because of the Nazis' dim view of unregulated theater). But acting gave way to another interest during the war. In 1942 he enrolled in an underground seminary being conducted in the archbishop's palace, and in November 1946 he was ordained a priest.

After earning a doctorate in ethics at the pontifical Angelicum University in Rome, where his chief academic mentor was a rigidly orthodox believer in Church tradition, he earned another in philosophy so that he could teach in Polish universities (which required such training). After a spell of teaching at Lublin and Cracow, he was consecrated bishop in 1958 and appointed archbishop of Cracow in 1964. Over the next eleven years his relations with the Communist government of Poland were correct but by no means subservient, a mixture of tension and mutual accommodation.

He participated actively in the Vatican II debates, in which his most widely publicized speech was an appeal for religious liberty—not within the Church but outside it, in contrast with earlier papal insistence that Catholicism must be the state religion everywhere. In the modern secular state, he argued, with its commitment to religious pluralism, the Church hardly can ask freedom for itself without favoring it for others. His rhetoric evidently brought him favorable attention, and this may have been a factor in his making cardinal in 1967 and in his eighth-ballot election to the papacy in October 1978, after the shockingly untimely death of John Paul I.

Another factor may have been his Ronald Reagan type of public amiability, which even the skeptical priest-sociologist-reporter Andrew Greeley credited with enabling a Pole to win over a jealous Italian public that had come to think of the papacy as a Roman preserve. His years as pope, the continually traveling pope, have revealed an extraordinary talent for public relations at the devotional level. He's clearly a charmer when he wants to be, and he has won the hearts of millions, probably tens or hundreds of millions. The significance of this need not be considered either good or bad. Charm, as history has often tragically shown us, can serve a variety of ends. Pope Alexander VI was one of the most charming of popes, and one of the most disastrous.

Hans Küng

Paul VI's encyclical *Humanae Vitae* offers an invaluable illustration of Rome's dilemma on the question, or assertion, of papal teaching authority. The prelates of the Roman Curia obviously are not confident enough in its strictures on birth control to declare them absolutely infallible, but they just as obviously want the sheep to consider them precisely that. For if the strictures are not infallible, then they are to some degree doubtful, and a venerable principle of Catholic moral theology is that a doubtful law is not binding. Thus the said prelates may be quite uncomfortable with the idea of papal infallibility, somewhat like more reasonable people if not in the same way.

Among the more reasonable people, the Swiss-born German theologian Hans Küng attracted worldwide attention in the early 1970s with a scholarly, perceptive and impudent book entitled *Infallibility? An Inquiry.* The title was a bit deceptive: beyond inquiring, the book recommended a view of infallibility designed to give curial cardinals cardiac conniptions. With regard to the

Church's teaching authority and function, Küng asserted, the Second Vatican Council might almost have never been held: "the ecclesiastical 'teaching office' is conceived by the Pope [Paul VI] and also by a number of bishops largely in a preconciliar authoritarian way," is expressed in a suffocating flow of apodictic, mostly fussy ukases, and is thereby putting greater stress on credibilty than Rome perhaps has ever known. As a recent and outstanding example he cited *Humanae Vitae,* which produced astonishment throughout the literate world as a curiosity dredged out of the Dark Ages and, within the Catholic communty, evoked not only shocked protest but also widespread, defiant noncompliance.

Therefore his inquiry concerning infallibility. First, as against Roman deduction, he resorted to inductive (historical) research, citing half a dozen teachings later repudiated or quietly reversed in practice, and suggesting also a "close scrutiny" of the late Index of Forbidden Books, that notorious brain-drainer. Although the "errors of the ecclesiastical teaching office in every century have been numerous and indisputable," official admissions of them have been niggardly and almost inaudible, lest such admissions lessen acceptance of authority. Lock-step theologians, especially after Vatican I, explained it all away with a "basically simple recipe": if the teaching was in error, then it was never (intended to be) infallible. Thus when some of the solemn teachings of Pope Honorius I were condemned (solemnly) by the Council of Constantinople and several later popes, it was because Honorius hadn't really meant them to be all that solemn. Deduction again: all solemn papal utterances are free from error, but (negatively) *these* utterances weren't free from error, so *they* couldn't have been solemn. (John XXIII once remarked, "I'm not infallible," but of course as was his wont, he wasn't being solemn.)

Humanae Vitae, however, was quite solemn and unequivocal, so that the epidemic of noncompliance among Catholic couples, the low opinions of the encyclical among Catholic priests, its bland indifference to inductive evidence, and its simple reliance on precedent, all raised questions about its authority amid the general discomfiture. Küng listed several: was this matter of birth control a proper subject for a dogmatic assertion, was the pope competent to interpret the "natural law" as well as revelation, did the pope really have such dogmatic authority alone (without the bishops), and wasn't this encyclical simply an expression of Paul's archreactionary prejudices? All these questions Küng dismissed, especially the last. Paul's condemnation of artificial birth control was a conscientious, courageous mistake.

But that did not mean that the pope had a monopoly on conscience. The encyclical provoked a renewed emphasis on the freedom of the individual conscience. "Those who, after serious and mature reflection, before themselves, their marriage partners and God, came to the conclusion that—for the maintenance of their love and the endurance and happiness of their marriage— they have to act in a way different from that which the encyclical lays down, are bound—according to the traditional teaching, also of the popes—to follow their conscience," continuing to receive the sacraments. But this subjective resolution of the problem for married couples, Küng added, did not address the objective question of papal infallibility.

Why did Paul do it? he asked. Because he could not bring himself to contradict or modify the declarations of his professionally, ostensibly celibate predecessors. Especially his recent predecessors, and most especially Pius XI, who issued a formidably purse-lipped encyclical on Christian marriage in 1930. *Humanae Vitae,* for instance, referred to church tradition some 25 times but to the gospels only twice. In response to the storm of controversy raised by the encyclical, Paul offered no evidence or argument in its defense but merely described what a burdensome decision it had entailed. As Küng put it elsewhere, the more seriously Rome takes its authority, the greater strain it seems to put on its credibility and on the unity of the Church.

Strain seems indeed to have been a feature of the deliberations of Paul's commission on birth control, with the majority clearly favoring contraception, the minority absolutely opposed to it, and the two arguing on different levels. The majority proposed that circumstances had changed enough since the days of Pius XI to justify a change in the teaching, especially since that encyclical need not be considered an infallible declaration. The minority, denying the changes, insisted that the teaching, infallible or not, was of too great importance and too long standing to be subject to change; after all, there had never been a formal, infallible pronouncement of the immorality of murder in the first degree, but a condemnation of murder was an age-old, integral part of Church teaching. Later Roman explanations of the minority view, after Paul had incorporated it into his encyclical, made it clear that a solemn papal pronouncement, firmly supported by tradition although perhaps technically fallible, was nonetheless to be accepted by the hapless faithful as an integral part of "the truth." Forever.

But a stunning proportion of the faithful, declining the

predicament of the hapless and abetted by considerable clerical and even some episcopal cooperation, have been paying recent popes' declarations on sex about as much attention as is usually given to laws against jaywalking. Given this low-keyed defiance of an irrational directive (whether true or not, it is irrational, offering no reasons but simply ordering, "Believe this because We say so"), and given the historical record of authoritative declarations, Küng asked, has the "problem of infallibility" really been "clarified once and for all?"

The history of official Church opinion, he conceded, clearly establishes the condemnation of contraception as a traditional, universal and thus presumably infallible teaching. Since the historical arguments are decisive, there are two possible reactions: "either, like the minority of the commission and the Pope, treat such teaching as infallible and irreversible and adhere to it despite all difficulties and objections, even, if necessary, sacrificing one's intellect; OR simply question this whole theory of infallibility."

There could be no appeal, he decided, to Vatican II. That council, although it earned a reputation for renewing and updating the Church, for rescuing it from its Roman bondage, cravenly knuckled under on the subject of papal infallibility. In its statement on the Church, the first two sections were scriptural, pastoral, tolerant; but its third section, on the hierarchy, essentially echoed the absolutist declaration of Vatican I. It did seem to draw a distinction between a traditional teaching, which must be "held," and a divinely revealed (scriptural) teaching, which must be "believed." This could make a difference to a preacher or a theological professor if "held" means something like "expressed," but it could hardly mean less to a conscientious Catholic married couple

27

stretched on the rack of *Humanae Vitae.* The council also added a comment on the proper response to Roman definitions, that "the assent of the Church can never be wanting"; this was written before the appearance of the notorious encyclical. (In ecclesiastical jargon "the Church" is used variously to apply to the whole Church, laity and all, or to any segment of it, especially the tiny segment headquartered in the Vatican. Distinctions are kept conveniently vague.)

As for Vatican I, that council was the ninth-inning climax of the centralizing of Catholicism which had begun some fifteen centuries earlier and had been greatly accelerated by Pope Gregory the Great and those of his successors who used the forgeries called the False Decretals so effectively in consolidating the primacy of the Roman see. By 1870, the year of Vatican I, Pius IX not only was standing at the end of a long line of power-absorbing predecessors; he also was the focus of much episcopal insecurity brought on by the Reformation, the Enlightenment, rationalism, positivism, liberalism, socialism, anticlericalism and other items that the pope eventually lumped together into the monster of "modernism" and frantically condemned in his historic *Syllabus of Errors.* The participants in Vatican I had reason to suffer from some degree of paranoia and to be motivated by it. Under these circumstances it is hardly surprising that they produced a council dedicated not to renewal but to reaction, or, as Küng put it, to "defense and polemics."

To investigate the reliability of its definition of papal infallibility, he continued, one must look back into the "prehistory" of the definition. "But it is not enough to expose this background critically and frankly—as Catholic historians do today—while at the same time refraining from any critical reflection on the definition itself." On not only its "opportuneness," that is, but also on "its very truth."

Before defining papal infallibility, Vatican I asserted papal "primacy," and in doing so it revealed the paranoid motivation mentioned above: "With daily increasing hatred, on all sides, the gates of hell are rising, to overturn the Church if it were possible, against its divinely established foundation. Therefore we judge it necessary for the protection, safety and increase of the Catholic flock, with the approval of the sacred council, to propose the doctrine of the institution, perpetuity and nature of the sacred apostolic primacy, in which the strength and solidity of the whole Church consists, to be believed and held by all the faithful. . . ." (No distinction appears here in the phrase "believed and held," presumably because of the scriptural basis for this proposal.)

From Peter's primacy in the New Testament the council inferred the primacy of "his successors," the Roman pontiffs, leaving to cooperative theologians the historical (inductive) details of the succession. This primacy, practically synonymous with "supremacy," led its more zealous proponents into paroxysms of submissiveness. Many held that the pope was continuously inspired by the Holy Spirit, some hailed him as "Vice-God," and one overstimulated bishop declared that he was God incarnate. But when the council came to defining his infallibility, the harassed minority managed to get some limits imposed, at least ostensibly: the infallibility would apply only to a formal declaration on a matter of faith or morals and would be distinguished from inspiration in being only a negative, ad-hoc protection from error. A pope naturally is expected to issue such declarations only for the good of the Church, but then only he can finally decide what is good for the Church. He is not obliged to consult anyone else, to seek any assistance, to do any research—to do anything, indeed, but open his mouth, and what he says *goes*. Nothing prevents him, strictly, from declaring Keynesian economics a matter of faith or morals, or from declaring inspiration and infallibility to be synonymous. Even King Louis XIV, Küng concluded, would have been quite satisfied with such a degree of power. The pope, he added, is the only absolute monarch to have survived the French Revolution.

The New Testament connection with the declaration of papal infallibility, he suggested, is debatable, as shown by the non-Catholic theologians who have been happy to debate it. The passages cited (Mt 16:18, Lk 22:32, Jn 22:15) speak of Peter as the rock on which to "build my church" and of his strengthening his brothers and feeding "my sheep," but there is no mention of anything resembling infallibility, or of successors, or of a bishop of Rome. Doubtless because of their ambiguity, the passages were not cited as proof of papal primacy until several centuries after Christ, much less as proof of infallibility, which did not become a front-burner issue until the 1800s. Something that Küng did not mention is that Jesus and his disciples seemed to expect an imminent end of the world, making the question of "succession" at most a peripheral consideration. (Jesus' knowledge was somehow limited, as he himself asserted.)

Then what of "tradition," or Church history—does it support a claim to papal infallibility? Not very solidly, Küng indicated, if at all. Indeed, the same could be said for, or against, papal supremacy, which effectively appeared only after Constantine opened the imperial door to Roman Catholicism but which even thereafter had to rely heavily on the Isidorian forgeries (the "False Decretals") for its precarious legitimacy. And the notion of papal infallibility derives little strength from the excommunication of Pope Vigilius in 553 or from the several condemnations of Pope Honorius I in 681 and thereafter.

By Luther's time, Küng pointed out, there still "was no unanimous opinion in the Church about the papal primacy (and its relationship to the council) or about the teaching authority of the pope." Even the Church-consolidating Council of Trent avoided these issues. But Cardinals Bellarmine, Torquemada and Cajetan used the authority of Thomas Aquinas, who in turn had used the False Decretals, to assert papal authority and thus pave the way for Vatican I.

Given this shaky background, Küng asserted, it seems clear why Vatican I resorted to comfortable generalities like "this the Holy See has always held" and "this the perpetual usage of the Church confirms." (Deduction again: an infallible Holy See and church *must* always have taught these things.) Inductively, the *"historical reality* looks different," especially during Christianity's first thousand years. But the council was not a collection of Church historians; it was a gathering of professional churchmen who felt besieged by a hostile world, who were charmed by the current pope's charisma and his lamentations over the hostility, and who decided to close ranks tightly around him without fussing about any minutes of past meetings. The majority's declaration of his infallibility thus arose out of wishful thinking presented as verifiable truth. Given that one believes in the Church as an indispensable leaven of truth (Mt 13:33), as Küng did and does, must the truth therefore be distributed in little packets, with every packet eternally, absolutely, indisputably true? Are these individually infallible propositions necessary to the reliability of the Church's teaching authority? Both Vatican I and Vatican II assumed this to be the case implicitly, but is such an assumption infallible?

Küng found it more questionable than infallible, partly because propositions, being made up of language, and in this case a dead language, are susceptible to its vicissitudes: incomplete communciation, misunderstandings, inadequate translations, changes in meaning with time, ideological manipulation. This problem was ignored by Vatican I because the neoscholasticism underlying that council largely accepted the rationalist belief in unmistakably clear assertions. The deficiencies of language thus leave propositions at the mercy of particular contexts, those hotbeds of misunderstandings—as when the Council of Trent condemned justification "by faith" as "by faith without good works" when the Reformers were thinking rather of faith *before* good works, a concept with which the Council could hardly have disagreed.

All this confronted Küng with a dilemma. On one horn were the promises reported in the New Testament such as "I will be with you always" and "I will send you the Spirit of Truth," and the reference in 1 Timothy 3:15 to the Church as upholding the truth and keeping it safe. On the other were the contradictions and other errors recorded by church historians, highlighted by later embarrassed, retroactive retractions of infallibility. A way out, he suggested, might be to admit the possibility of error in particular propositions while accepting the general significance of the promises: the Church's teaching will be true in spite of any errors cropping up in individual teachings now and then. It might be called "indefectible" rather than "infallible," or "perpetually true" rather than "infallibly true."

In Pope Paul's commission on birth control, the anti-contraception minority argued that approval of artificial birth control would deny Rome's long-held position, and for "the Church to have erred so gravely in its grave responsibility of leading souls would be tantamount to seriously suggesting that the assistance of the Holy Spirit was lacking to her." (The "her" refers to Mother Church.) Oh, ye of little faith, Küng responded, don't you believe that the Holy Spirit would survive? Are Rome and the Holy Spirit one and the same? What is needed is a faith that "will not identify, but distinguish between, the Spirit of God and the Church [and] will be able to see without illusions that the Church's development always includes wrong developments and her progress always includes setbacks." He seemed almost to be paraphrasing Lord Macauley's comment to the effect that the Catholic Church must have a solid core of divine truth to have survived its disreputable history. Indeed, if the Lord could put up for all those centuries with the mercurial and obstreperous Hebrews of the old covenant, surely he, or she, can endure the buffoonery in the new.

It requires much less than Kierkegaard's "leap of faith" to discern the Holy Spirit protecting the Church from its enemies in the papacy during, say, those notorious tenth and fifteenth centuries, when its indefectibility was manifested not "in the hierarchy and not in theology, but among those innumerable and mostly unknown Christians—and there were always some bishops and theologians also among them—who, even in the Church's worst periods, heard the Christian message and tried to live according to it in faith, love, and hope."

Küng's proposal was a very Protestant one. He went so far as to quote Calvin, not the best selection for currying Roman favor: "I am quite convinced that truth does not die in the church, even though it be oppressed by one council, but is wonderfully preserved by the Lord, so that it may rise up and triumph again in its own time. But I *deny* it to be *always* the case that an interpretation of Scripture adopted by *vote of a council is true and certain.*" Yet this Protestant tinge, he maintained, might prove useful in a genuine effort to reunify Christianity. If *Humanae Vitae,* in so many respects "a misfortune for the Catholic Church," should "turn out to be a catalyst, to hasten reflection on ecclesiastical infallibility," it might be just what the ecumenical movement needs.

Certainly ecumenism receives no nourishment from the aggressive insistence on the papacy as the source of all authority. Appealing to St. Paul's references to people's various talents (1 Cor 7:7,17; 12:29), Küng pleaded for recognition of the distinction between the leadership function of the papacy and the scholarship-teaching function of theologians. In this he was echoing the plea of the 1360 theologians who in 1968, in some alarm, publicly cautioned that "the freedom of theologians and theology in the service of the church, regained by Vatican II, must not now be jeopardized again." Teaching authority surely resides in the Church as a whole, he protested: "From all that has had to be said in this book, from beginning to end, it is clear that the

Holy Spirit is not given only to pope and bishops in authentic fashion for the salvation of the Church, that the Church is by no means identical with the Church's leaders, that the truth of the Christian faith is not 'deposited' in Roman offices and episcopal chancelleries, that the 'authentic' proclamation and exposition of the Christian message is not 'reserved' to anyone. The Spirit of God breathes where he will; he is greater than the Church and the Church is greater than her leadership."

*   *   *

Almost a decade later, in 1979, Küng reaffirmed his views in a more succinct and very thin volume, *The Church—Maintained in Truth?* That year he also wrote the preface to a less than obsequious book by August Hasler entitled *How the Pope Became Infallible.* Hasler's book seems to have been totally eclipsed by the preface and the Roman reaction to it. The Congregation for the Doctrine of the Faith evidently thought that Küng had receded into the state of docility they know and love, but now here he was again, complicating their work of protecting the catatonic faithful from world, flesh and devil. (Especially flesh. Nasty business, that.)

They were right about his complicating their work, which would be so much simpler if everyone would just cultivate such cardinal virtues as blind obedience, bowing, scraping, ring-kissing, genuflecting, and reverent inaudibility. For in the preface, in reviewing the decade of discussion since the appearance of *Infallible?*, he concluded that the situation had grown considerably looser. Asking searching questions about infallibilty was less of a hair-raising activity among Catholic theologians, who manifestly had grown weary of explaining and qualifying and refashioning the Vatican I declaration against its background of historical impertinence ("Oh, but Pope Honorius wasn't really speaking infallibly!"). At least such questioning was growing more frequent. He also detected a wider acceptance of the proposition that particular papal teachings could be mistaken without obliterating all teaching authority, although what he really detected may have been a wider recognition of his point about the inadequacies of language, leading to diminished confidence in the usefulness of the whole idea of infallibility. And he added an unexpected nose-tweaker, asserting that theologians were backing away from using the conventional New Testament passages and early Church tradition as reliable sources of support for papal and even conciliar infallibility—which historians of the medieval Church now described as an innovation of the thirteenth century, devised by a Franciscan friar, Peter Olivi, whom Pope John XXII later condemned as a diabolical liar. Under these circumstances, Küng proposed, an ecumenical commission should be appointed to study the question of infallibility.

In identifying himself with Hasler's book he may have been inviting guilt by association. Hasler's position was that the participants in Vatican I were manipulated by the iron-willed and irascible Pius IX, who was convinced of his infallibility by ecstatic visions that raised questions about his mental stability. Hasler apparently was muffled at the diocesan level, but the Küng case needed more elaborate treatment from headquarters.

And so in December 1979 the CDF solemnly declared, "Küng has departed from the integral truth of the Catholic faith and therefore can no longer be considered as a Catholic theologian nor function as such in a teaching role." His notion of "indefect-ibility" was proscribed for allowing "the possibility of error in doctrinal statements which the *magisterium* of the Church teaches must be held definitively." This prompted the German bishops to concur publicly with the condemnation and to withdraw their permission for him to teach theology at the University of Tübingen.

He had not defended himself in Rome. The Vatican Press office reported that he had declined "repeated invitations to participate in a discussion" of the matter, but the invitations included the customary stipulations: he would not know of any accusations in advance, nor would his accusers be identified; his defending counsel would be a Vatican official unknown to him; and he would have no right of appeal. The invitations thus seemed to him more like summonses to a Kafkaesque meat-grinder, and so he decided not to travel for his health. To the condemnation he reacted vigorously, angrily. As a Catholic theologian, he would "continue to fight for Catholics and not give in until this decision has been revoked." He deplored the "inquisitorial procedures" of a Church founded by Christ and engaged in the human rights movement, and was ashamed at the collaboration of the German bishops.

His own bishop loyally and bravely appealed directly to John Paul and was granted an audience, but it resulted simply in a confirmation of the original declaration. This forced the bishop to request the provincial ministry of education to take the final step of firing Küng and replacing him with someone more docile. Meanwhile protests were being voiced all over the world, though evidently at frequencies to which Vatican hearts were not attuned, from hundreds of German leaders, clerical and lay, from fifty Spanish theologians, from seventy American theologians, and so on. The Americans, true to their devilish tradition of free speech, insisted that, even though they might not agree with all Küng's opinions, he was nonetheless "indeed a Catholic theologian." But they were muttering into a wall. Although he was still a priest, allowed to perform ordinary priestly duties, theologically and officially he had become a nonperson.

Perhaps as a result of the discomfiting publicity, Rome later accepted an uneasy compromise that allowed the upstart to continue as professor of ecumenical theology and as chairman of committees in Tübingen's Catholic Theology Faculty. This ostensibly maintained his status both as a secular teacher and as a Catholic-theological nonperson. It could not have been a very satisfying arrangement for him, nor for those Romans who doubtless were sniffing the anticipated aroma of the stake. But at least it conceded some separation between church and state. And it has evidently done his reputation no harm whatsoever, since his theological opinions remain uncompromised.

He has been criticized by friendly colleagues for couching those opinions in a sometimes harsh, provocative style; indeed, words like "totalitarian" do occasionally crop up in his writing. It would seem naive, however, to ascribe Rome's attempt at stoppage to mere style. He is telling John Paul & Co. that they are smoking rope when they declare a pope's solemnly promulgated opinions to be indisputable, "irreformable." He might have tried disguising this assertion in soft language, but some of the prelates surely are bright enough, and more of them surely are perk-sensitive enough, to catch on to the fact that he is undermining what they hold as their very reason for being.

In this respect they must be terribly insecure: it is notable that they have simply ignored his (and others') inductive argument based on historical evidence of demonstrable errors in solemn declarations of the past. They cower behind their circular deduction: All solemn papal teaching is infallible; the declaration of papal infallibility is papal teaching; therefore it is infallible, irreformable, unchangeable, unassailable, and everything else reassuring.

Poor Hans Küng. John Paul, only eight years older than he, is likely to be ensconced on that seat of wisdom for a very long time. This is especially unfortunate because the Romans (including the Pole) have painted themselves into a corner, and Küng has been desperately trying to show them a way out. But he has been laboring under the impression that, like reasonable people, they are uncomfortable there. Apparently he is wrong. They seem to like it there just fine.

* * *

Hans Küng was born in March 1928 in the free, democratic air of Switzerland. After receiving a conventional liberal-arts education in Lucerne, at the age of twenty he went to Rome, where he attended the Pontifical German College and the Pontifical Gregorian University, majoring in philosophy and theology. His studies included side trips to London, Amsterdam, Berlin, Madrid and Paris. (Like John Paul, he is a linguist, with competence in German, Latin, Greek, Hebrew, French, English,

Spanish, Italian and Dutch.) His years as a student were both stimulating and disillusioning; stimulating because several of his teachers were noted scholars later silenced by Rome, disillusioning because of Rome's efforts against such popular movements as ecumenism, the "new theology," and France's worker-priests. Pious Pius XII, whom he had admired, had managed—with his endless outpouring of encyclicals, addresses, letters, etc.—to "demythologize" himself. Also, near the close of his stay in Rome, he was appointed chaplain to the Italian workers at the German College, and his attempts to improve their lot met with a determined resistance, indicating that Church reform might be needed in more ways than one.

Three years after his ordination as priest in 1954, he earned his doctorate in theology from the Catholic Institute at the Sorbonne, where he revealed his early and enduring interest in Christian reunion by writing his dissertation on the towering Protestant theologian Karl Barth. On the Christian doctrine of justification, he proposed, Barth's and the Catholic Council of Trent's views fundamentally agreed in principle. The thesis, published in a book that proved rather sensational, was well received by both Catholic and Protestant theologians, and Barth himself was sufficiently impressed to write the introduction to the American edition, published in 1963. Apparently it almost made it into the *Index of Forbidden Books*.

After a brief spell of parish work and teaching, Küng in 1960 was appointed full professor of fundamental theology at Germany's University of Tübingen and not long thereafter became co-editor of the university's theological quarterly, the oldest of Catholic theological journals. That year he also published *The*

Council, Reform and Reunion, which, in urging renewal à la John XXIII, earned him a place at Vatican II as a theological consultant. In 1962, the council's first year, his *Structures of the Church* examined Rome's authority in the light of unflattering history, and for this he was summoned to his first brush with the Roman bureaucracy. But the bureaucrats goofed by allowing his mentor, Cardinal Bea, of Germany, to chair the proceedings, and no action was taken against him.

In 1963 he was invited to the United States for a lecture tour. His name was on a list of proposed speakers for some Lenten lectures at Catholic University in Washington, D.C., a school with treasured papal connections. From this list the rector circumspectly removed the names of four highly respected theologians not much given to cringing or fawning: John Courtney Murray, Gustave Weigel, Godfrey Dikemann, and Küng. Circumspection lost out to a press leak, however, and news of the pusillanimous omissions hit the journalistic fan, meanwhile revealing many other instances of similar repression and generally creating a high-temperature furor. Küng was also refused episcopal permission to speak in several cities, including Los Angeles, San Diego, St. Paul and Philadelphia. Where he did speak, however, it was strictly Standing Room Only. After all, he was arguing for greater recognition of the individual conscience, for a Church declaration of the right to freedom of worship, for elimination of the Index, for revamping of the Holy Office's methods of dealing with heresy and other deviationism—in America, land of the free.

In April 1967 his book, *The Church,* was published, and the Congregation for the Doctrine of the Faith promptly reprimanded the bishop of Rottenburg for giving it an imprimatur.

This was the German edition, followed over the next two years by English, French, American, Spanish, Italian and Portuguese editions. Rome pursued its instinct for suppression rather belatedly: through the nuncio in Seoul, it finally managed to stop publication of a Korean edition.

In another respect, however, it ran truer to form, sending Küng a summons, which he received on May 4, 1968, to report in Rome for "a discussion" on the 9th, as though he had nothing else to do. Despite this unpromising start—he replied that he couldn't simply drop everything on such short notice—the exchanges over the next couple of years were not unfriendly, although he did keep insisting on unprecedented concessions like access to his dossier, a list of the accusations and accusers, and inquisitors competent in his field. He did not flatly refuse to go to Rome, but delays and other commitments complicated the process, and eventually the Romans seemed to lose interest, apparently becoming preoccupied with the pursuit of easier prey. Before they could return to his case he had published *Infallible?*, which gave their proscribing new vigor and focus.

This time the exchanges, for all their formal endearments, were not so friendly. Between February 1971 and February 1975 letters of stupifying length and complexity passed between Rome and Germany, dealing not with infallibility but with the procedures to be followed in the inquisition. The controversy soon spilled out into the media at both ends, reverberating with charges and countercharges. Amid all the noise the only reference to the central question of infallibility was in the Roman reply to the upstart's request for a reasonable argument in support of "the possibility of infallibility." In March 1974 the CDF refused to play that risky game, explaining that "the competence of the Congregation extends to the teaching of the faith" and not to arguing about it because the CDF "is not a theological faculty but rather an organ in the service of the teaching office of the Pope." So, as was to be expected, the Congregation, in its declaration of February 1975—announcing that the case was closed "for now" and admonishing Küng "not to advocate these doctrines" on infallibility—supported its opinion on the subject simply with a reference to the declarations of the two Vatican Councils.

The German Bishops' Conference only two days later welcomed the admonition enthusiastically in a public statement. Citing his previous books as well as his latest, *On Being a Christian,* they deplored his insubordinate deviations from the straight and narrow and advised him to watch his step. Here he was, they complained, demanding "from the ecclesiastical teaching office 'proof' which precisely the theologian should bring forth. Here a reversal in principle of the relationship of a Catholic theologian to the tradition of the faith of his Church is threatened." In short, whatever Rome's opinion may be today, your job is to come up with proofs for it, and, if it changes tomorrow, to come up with proofs for *that*. This has a familiar ring, recalling the predicament of scholars in Nazi Germany and the Soviet Union. (Any pious response that Rome's opinion can't change tomorrow simply relies on blind faith at the expense of history.)

One of Küng's steadiest supporters, although often an uneasy one because of the theologian's prickly obstinacy, was the Archbishop of Munich and President of the Bishops' Conference, Cardinal Julius Dopfner. In July 1976 he died and was replaced by Cardinal Joseph Ratzinger in Munich and by Cardinal Joseph

LOUIS BALDWIN

Hoffner as Conference President. Their shared attitude toward rambunctious theologians was somewhat to the right of the Conference statement issued the year before. Ratzinger, especially after his later appointment by John Paul as head of the CDF, would earn world-wide notoriety as a hard-nosed reactionary, the Vatican's relentless bird dog in the ceaseless hunt for error.

Over the next couple of years the relationship between Küng and the German bishops was approximately that between a fly and a clumsily wielded flyswatter, but something occurred in Rome that would bring new effectiveness to the swatting program. In August 1978 the conscientiously indecisive Paul VI died and, after the brief incumbency of John Paul I, Cardinal Karol Wojtyla became John Paul II in October. The new pope had the same regard for theologians as the German bishops, expressed particularly in a 1971 address to the Polish Congress of Theology and to be underlined in an October 1979 papal speech to the International Theological Commission.

As a present for Christmas Küng sent John Paul a copy of his latest book, *Does God Exist?*, and three months later had the effrontery to address a letter to him personally, a letter accompanied by a copy of his still later book, *The Church—Maintained in Truth?* The letter pleaded for reconsideration of Rome's attitudes toward contraception, the status of women, the "validity of Anglican and Protestant offices and eucharistic celebrations," and clerical celibacy. There was no reply: John Paul evidently retreated into that stony silence with which he has regularly greeted failures in adulation during his travels about the world.

In the fall of 1979 Küng wrote an assessment of the pope's

44

first year in office. Also failing in adulation and appearing in several major newspapers throughout the world, it reportedly attracted serious papal attention, laced with resentment. Soon thereafter the three German cardinals, during a Vatican visit, met with the pope in private audience. On their return to Germany one of them, Ratzinger, began making threatening noises for the first time: Küng "no longer represents the faith of the Catholic Church. . . and therefore cannot speak in its name." The cardinal also hinted at withdrawing Küng's permission to teach, and about a month later the withdrawal notice arrived from Rome. Some two days later came the German bishops' lengthy statement of concurrence. *Semper parati.*

The year 1979 had been a gratifyingly busy one for Roman doctrinaires. On April 3 Jacques Pohier, a Dominican professor at the Catholic Institute in Paris, was ordered to shut up and stop saying mass because of the "evident errors" and "dangerous statements" which some CDF bureaucrat had sniffed out in his book *Quand Je Dis Dieu.* That same day John Paul warned students and teachers in Roman schools of theology that what the Church needed was "priests who build up and do not tear down when teaching faith and morals," doubtless in the tradition of Alexander VI, among others. In August the CDF condemned *Human Sexuality,* a book by half a dozen members of the Catholic Theological Society of America, for proposing that procreation is "not essential to sexuality." In September John Paul demanded more rigorous obedience from the Jesuits and later, during his visit to the United States, amid all the meticulously scheduled adulation, raised many a ruckus by occasionally sounding like a doctrinal Genghis Khan, particularly on women, sex and celibacy. In October William Callahan, S.J., was disciplined for supporting the idea of women in the priesthood, and Robert Drinan, S.J., Congressman from Massachusetts, was forbidden to hold elective office. And in December, to round things out, Edward Schillebeeckx, the Dutch theologian, was grilled at the Vatican on charges of deviationism in Christology. It was a very invigorating year.

The protest against Rome's suppression of Küng was immediate, loud, voluminous, world-wide, and various in form, viewpoint and source. He himself received 5,000 letters of support. Millions of words were written in private letters and public statements. Organizations were formed "for the rights of Catholics"— for the recognition of such rights not by the Soviet Union but by the Vatican. It was not that all the protestors, or even most, agreed with his arguments. His writing can be abstruse, verbose, risky—as in his precarious reliance on the Hegelian dialectic in questioning the usefulness of "propositions." It was rather (shades of Voltaire) that he had a right to say what he thought as a Catholic theologian without having his elementary right to a fair hearing simply ignored. Or, as Patrick McGrath put it in Britain's *The Tablet,* what was being demanded was a reasonable refutation. "If this can be provided, then a condemnation is unnecessary; if it cannot be provided, then a condemnation is unjustified."

The verdict of Küng's theological peers, although mixed with regard to his opinions, was virtually unanimous concerning the shabby treatment of someone who, through his writing, has surely won the church more friends than any hundred Roman prelates. A very few of his critics were so exultant as to welcome any means of getting rid of him. A notable example was Archbishop

Lefebvre, the only one to introduce the word "heretic" into the controversy, although he himself had been squelched by Rome (although rather gently, by John Paul himself) for his reactionary views on the liturgy. But these exceptions were drowned out in the din of protest.

The effect on Küng's popularity at the University of Tübingen was striking. Before his ostracism his lectures had been attended by something over a hundred students. After it, in his new status as a secular employee of the university (where attendance at lectures was never required), his lectures filled his 300-seat classroom and were piped into an adjacent hall also holding 300 students. This was during the spring term, 1980; in the fall he had to be moved because he was regularly drawing a thousand or so. In addition, during his eleven-day tour of the United States that November he lectured to consistently packed houses.

Meanwhile, in May, John Paul had written the German bishops a letter congratulating them on their condemnation of the deviant and on their cooperation with "the Congregation for the Doctrine of the Faith, whose duty—always essential to the life of the Church [sic—since about 35 A.D.]—seems to be in our time particularly burdened with responsibility and difficulty." In the church, he went on, there must be "authentic dialogue," but to this dialogue Rome brings "that which it has received based on certainty"; so much for authentic dialogue. The deviant has said "that he wishes to be and remains a Catholic theologian. In his works, however, he manifests clearly that he does not consider several authentic [and still unspecified] doctrines of the Church as definitively decided and binding on himself and his theology." And so he must not indulge in "the oral and written expression" of his opinions.

Jesus Christ, John Paul continued, gave the Church "the gift of a specific 'infallibility,'" and anyone who questions it "separates the Church from him who, as the bridegroom, 'loved' it and gave himself for it." (The quotation marks around "loved" were not explained.) In view of the mission with which Christ entrusted the Church, "could he possibly have deprived it of the certainty of professed and proclaimed truth?" (This is the question to which Küng had answered no in his argument for "indefectibility" or "perpetuity in truth.") The ovine need for certainty is the letter's thesis, arising out of the classic Roman paranoia over the "tempests" raging against the embattled Church. "The Church must confront these storms and cannot be affected by uncertainty in faith and by relativism of truth and morals." Only such certainty "is able to oppose the radical negations of our time" disseminated "by propaganda and pressure." As for the "ecumenical work of Christian unity," the duty of Catholic theologians, in their dialogue with any "separated brethren," is to remain "faithful to the doctrine of the Church." Of Rome, that is.

The epistle from John Paul to the Germans ended most piously. "Love requires that we seek a meeting in truth with every person. Therefore, we do not cease to implore God for such a meeting in a particular way with this man, our brother. . . ." Küng, mistaking this for a genuine invitation, replied by expressing his gratitude and suggesting that such a meeting could take some of the sting out of some pressing and divisive problems in the Church. His letter went unanswered. He had evidently failed to notice that this was to be a meeting "in truth" and "in a particular way."

Edward Schillebeeckx

Most Catholic theologians, being priests, are preachers. As such they generally suffer from occupational verbosity, aggravated by high-flown obscurity. John Paul has an extremely severe case. Hans Küng, with a milder case, is often downright intelligible. Somewhere in between is the Flemish theologian Edward Schillebeeckx (pronounced approximately *Skila*bakes), a Dominican priest whose soft and vagrant prose seems to invite inference more often than understanding. This may seem a very subjective judgment, but (as he and Küng might say in other connections) the historical fact is that, after issuing his two "Jesus books" in 1974 and 1977 (with English versions in 1979 and 1980), he had to write another book in 1981 in a valiant effort to clear up the misunderstandings. And his summons to Rome was not for summary condemnation but for "clarification."

That summons came from inquisitors who had been alerted to his first Jesus book, *Jesus: An Experiment in Christology* (or, in the more appropriately titled Dutch edition, *Jesus: The*

Story of a Life). He wrote it because the religious environment
in which the New Testament originated is so different from ours
today. For instance, we "do not live in a cultural-religious tradition
that expects a messiah or a mysterious, celestial son of man:
nor do we live in expectation of an approaching end of the
world." And so what "does salvation in Jesus, coming to us
from God, mean to us now?"

It can hardly mean, he answered, what it meant to first-
century Christians. For one thing, the competition seems so much
more pressing today: science and technology are widely looked
on as a source of salvation for mankind, despite some spectacular
failures, and non-Christian religions of worldwide repute offer
alternative routes (as in California?). Amid the competition,
however, Jesus seems to hold a strong attraction for many non-
Christians and even for nonreligious people, who seem reluctant
to renounce all hope of something beyond the here and now.
Meanwhile within Christianity a division has arisen between an
interest in the earthbound Jesus and an absorption in the risen
Christ. All these phenomena impose on the theologian a demand
for an underpinning of faith with reason, in this case with history
(of deduction with induction?). An important addendum is the
age-old hostility of Christians toward Jews, those victims of
misdirected faith. "Faith and historical criticism go hand in hand,
therefore, on almost every page of this book."

What we know of Jesus is the effect he had on his followers.
The gospels are history, Schillebeeckx maintained, but "as interpreted in the language of faith," for what Jesus left behind was
not a book but a movement. This gives rise to the problem of
distinguishing the historical Jesus from the Jesus of the move-

ment, with its "religious and cultural expectations, aspirations and ideologies." For in a sense there was more than one Jesus, as can be seen in the Jewish-Christian Messiah and the Greek-Christian Lord. Since his departure from this mortal coil (and indeed even before it) he has appeared in many images, under many titles, such as Son of Man, Son of God, Light of Light, the Way of the Cross, the Fount of Faith, Christ the King, the Infant Jesus, the Sacred Heart, the Jesus of human liberation. The human tendency to refashion him must be restrained by historical inquiry lest we "turn Jesus into a mere receptable for our own predilections." Such inquiry cannot supplant faith in the risen Christ the Savior, but modern historical criticism has revealed a reliable continuity between that Christ and the Jesus who suffered under Pontius Pilate, thus "making up, concretely, the content of faith," somewhat as a reliable biography of Elizabeth Tudor supports the history of that extraordinary Queen of England.

The emphasis that emerges from the myriad details of such scrutiny—and from long chapters with such unnerving titles as "A Conjunctural Horizon of Ideas and Non-Synchronous Rhythm in the Complex Transformation of a Culture" and "Necessary, Problematic Character and Limits of a Theoretical-cum-Christological Identification of the Person"—is on Jesus' "*Abba* experience," his awareness of the fatherhood of God as it uniquely applied to him in the saving mission that culminated in his death and resurrection.

Since a father in this instance necessarily implies a son, Schillebeeckx at this point had to discuss Jesus as the Second Person of the Blessed Trinity. After a long consideration of the many views on the meaning of "person," he wound up with statements like this: "The constitutive relation to God resides already in the core of each creature as being and person. Thus, thanks to the hypostatic identification of that in God which because of Jesus we call 'Son of God' with Jesus' personal-cum-human mode of being, the man Jesus is a constitutive (filial) relation to the Father, a relation that in the dynamic process of Jesus' human life grows into a deepening, mutual *enhypostasis,* with the resurrection as its climactic point." What seems to be the book's coda displayed a similar crystal clarity, although the dead-end quality of the sentence sounds clear enough: "How the man Jesus can be for us at the same time the form and aspect of a present divine 'person,' the Son, transcending our future through an overwhelming immanence, is in my view, despite the non-contradiction that we recognize and the fact that Jesus of Nazareth's living of it has made sense of it, a mystery unfathomable at this point."

With assertions like these, surely unobjectionable to all but the most determined inquisitorial ferret, the book might well have caused hardly a theological ripple. But he had called attention to himself in 1966 with his contribution to the heatedly controversial Dutch catechism, and then, during a U.S. lecture tour in 1967, with some dangerously ambiguous remarks about the appeal of traditional Christian revelation in modern society, so that a Schillebeeckx dossier had already been started in the Roman files on potential deviants by the time the book appeared. It is surely significant that, when he was called to Rome for questioning about the book in December 1979, the first topic on the interrogation list was "the nature of divine revelation," which he had mentioned in his American lectures but not in the book.

There were other topics on the list, but it soon became clear that the central issue binding them together was the question of his adherence to the Chalcedonian formula for the divinity of Christ. By the early 400s the popular devotion to Mary had grown fervent enough to become controversial. Her most ardent admirers had entitled her "Mother of God" and needed some official support for that extraordinary moniker. The support came in the form of a declaration by the Council of Chalcedon in 451 that Jesus Christ was true God and true man, with two natures, divine and human, distinct yet totally united in one person, quite paradoxically and mysteriously. The basic question for Schillebeeckx was, did he subscribe to the divinity of Christ? And, if he did, how would he go about clarifying his position?

Unlike Küng, he responded to his summons by going to Rome, naively assuming that he would be treated courteously. In a superficial sense, he was; indeed, even he became wary of the fulsome cordiality displayed by people who even he knew had a less than obsessive interest in his serenity. He was assured, however, as were the media, that this was not a trial that he had been summoned to, but rather a "procedure." The nomenclature was derived from an age-old premise, most recently cultivated extensively by Ronald Reagan & Co.: "Anything is anything I say it is." Or perhaps Rome inadvertently neglected to include the definitive adjective, as in "star-chamber procedure." In any case, the "procedure" entailed secret accusations, unidentified accusers, primed inquisitors, oral examinations, and a decision from which there could be no appeal.

The summons raised a storm of protest from Catholic and non-Catholic theologians, university faculties, priests, nuns and laypeople in Europe and the Americas. Schillebeeckx, they argued, had contributed enormously not only to ecumenism but also to a contemporary understanding of Christianity. Surely a condemnation of his work would hurt the Church more severely than any unorthodox material it might contain, especially if the proceedings against him were conducted with the medieval rigor that had already earned Rome such notoriety.

How much effect the protests had on the Romans, if any, is unknown. One group of Amsterdam theological students had a petition with 60,000 signatures hand-carried to the Vatican, where it promptly disappeared into the archival maw. Protests and petitions were quite irrelevant. The central question remained: do this man's opinions conform to our opinions of the Chalcedon formula? How severely his work could be scrutinized might be inferred from a remark by the late Cardinal Ottaviani. A theologian employed by the CDF when Ottaviani headed it reported that the Cardinal had said on one occasion that even St. Paul "would not have been able to meet our stern requirements of clarity and absence of ambiguity."

Schillebeeckx had already been found unable "to meet our stern requirements." Some thirty months earlier, in April 1977, he had received a questionnaire from the Congregation containing some of the charges that had been leveled against his book, and asking for his replies. His response was a detailed, 8000-word answer explaining that the book was only the first of three volumes; that the charges predominantly concerned omissions of material to be treated, more appropriately, in the second and third volumes; that many or most of the charges resulted from misunderstandings, some accusing him of holding the exact opposite of what he had written. On the central point he protested that he had explicitly supported the Chalcedon doctrine as "straight gospel" while also asserting that "such notions as 'hypostasis, nature and person' . . . no longer have the same meaning that they had at the time of Chalcedon" fifteen centuries before. Thus a major purpose of the book was "precisely to translate the dogma of Chalcedon into the language of the faithful today."

His explanation was rejected in July 1978, and a tentative summons to a "discussion" was issued for October. But that summer saw the death of two popes and the election of a third, and so the focus on Schillebeeckx blurred again for another year. Meanwhile the CDF launched an eyes-heavenward PR campaign—including its first-ever press release—to counter the protests. This was no witch-hunt but was rather a friendly, pastoral conversation for the purpose of clarification. Rome had a duty to protect "the right of the faithful to receive sound and authentic doctrine." Those simple ignoramuses had a right to information right from the horse's mouth, and there must be only one horse, a horse of certified pedigree.

But the horse in this instance turned out to be of another color, a color more political than doctrinal. Schillebeeckx was scheduled for his inquisition on December 13, 14 and 15. On December 4 a Jesuit doctrinaire in Vatican service, who ten days later would turn up as one of the secret inquisitors, was interviewed in a Vatican Radio broadcast. In answer to a question involving Schillebeeckx, he commented on theologians who "deny the divinity of Christ." This revelation of prejudice was clear enough for the director of Vatican Radio, another Jesuit, to apologize to Dominican Schillebeeckx soon afterward. But it may have had a more important consequence.

Cardinal Johannes Willebrands had been the archbishop of Utrecht, and thus Schillebeeckx's ecclesiastical superior, for only a short time. He was also President of the Dutch Episcopal Conference, Chancellor of the Catholic University of Nijmegen (Schillebeeckx's home base), President of the Vatican's Secretariat for Christian Unity, and one of the cardinals in the CDF. He had become a big man on the ecclesiastical campus partly by knowing when to keep his mouth shut. But on December 11, 1979, he opened his mouth very audibly, perhaps inspired by the airborne big-mouthing of the week before. On a Dutch radio program he announced his support for Schillebeeckx as a profoundly knowledgeable theologian. "I have a high regard for Schillebeeckx. His teaching is the fruit of his Christian faith and his dedication to the Church. There are few theologians in the Church who are on his level. He is dear to me because of his faith and his service to the Church." Nor was this all: "I hope that the Schillebeeckx case will be resolved favorably. But if it comes before the cardinals of the CDF, I promise to be present at the meeting and to defend him."

Apparently no formal defense ever was necessary, perhaps because of this stout informal defense. The case was left hanging, going no further than "clarification." On December 15, the secretary of the CDF told Schillebeeckx that the decision doubtless would take some time. Eventually the harassed theologian was told simply to "clear up ambiguities" in his writing in the future. Since these were *future* ambiguities, they were left ambiguously unidentified. Apparently the weather had calmed down in the teapot.

EDWARD SCHILLEBEECKX

*   *   *

Of the fourteen Schillebeeckx children the sixth, Edward, was
born in November 1914 in Antwerp, Belgium, in the northern,
Flemish part of the country. As a teenager he nearly followed
an older brother to India to join the Jesuit missions. His motivation, however, was prophetic: it was not so much a desire to
do missionary work as to investigate Hinduism and Buddhism,
and especially their similarities to Christianity. Since such an
investigation really did not require a trip to India, he stayed
home instead and did a lot of reading. Evidently he liked reading
better than traveling, enough at any rate to choose the relatively
quiet groves of academe and the Dominican Order of Preachers
over the more strenuous, competitive Society of Jesus.

Accepted by the Dominican house of studies in Ghent, he
studied philosophy there for three years, at the end of which
he was conscripted for military service. During his hitch he spent
much of his spare time reading philosophy, laced with some
sociology and psychology. After it he continued his philosophy
studies at the Catholic University of Louvain, which included
a Dominican college of theology. As he entered into theology,
he found the heavy hand of neo-Thomism less than inspiring.
His master of studies recommended the more modern theologian
Karl Adam (1876-1966) as an alternative.

Adam, who was teaching dogmatic theology at the University
of Tübingen in Germany, was noted for reaching back beyond
Aquinas to Augustine and the early church, and especially to
the Bible, for his inspiration. In Adam's *Christ Our Brother* and
The Spirit of Catholicism Schillebeeckx discovered that a theo-

logian could discuss "all the dogmas of the Church from the Trinity to the Immaculate Conception without using a single scholastic term in all his work." He went on to make similarly bracing discoveries in the work of other unregimented theologians like Pierre Rousselot, Yves Congar and Karl Rahner.

Ordained in 1941, he was sent to Paris to study at the Sorbonne and at the French Dominican house of studies, which awarded him his doctorate in theology. In Paris he was influenced by Abbé Chenu, a Dominican interested in relating the Church more closely to contemporary problems, especially social problems, foreshadowing what today is called liberation theology. From Chenu, who was unsurprisingly condemned by Rome, he also learned "how to carry on when you are under suspicion."

In 1943 he became a theology professor at the University of Louvain. As the forties slipped into the fifties, he found an increasing number of his students interested in, and indeed eager to join, the French priest-worker movement, in which priests worked and lived very much as did their parishioners, and which was later condemned. To develop an appropriate theology for such a mission, he joined his students on occasion in social work, spending a summer with them, for example, in building a center for refugees near the border of East Germany and helping with resettlement efforts. At the end of each workday he and the students gathered together for theological discussion and reflection, becoming "a very close community."

Beginning in 1947 he headed the four-year dogmatic theology program at Louvain for ten years, teaching a great variety of courses. In the early fifties he published a book on the sacraments and another on Mary, taking unconventional but apparently not conspicuously controversial approaches to those subjects. His approach as his students' spiritual counselor was also unconventional *and* rather controversial, being alarmingly progressive and permissive. Faculty mossbacks doubtless were delighted by his departure, in 1947, for the University of Nijmegen, where he would teach theology for the next quarter century.

During Vatican II, which lasted from 1962 to 1965, he was in Rome as theological consultant to the delegation of Dutch bishops. His book on marriage, published in 1963, may have been the chief reason for his assignment as one of the three theologians who wrote the final draft of the section on marriage and the family in the council's document, "The Church in the Modern World." Like many others, he was greatly heartened by the new candor, tolerance, collegiality and open-mindedness displayed by the council in its early sessions. His disappointment in the final outcome was therefore all the more severe. He was appalled by Paul VI's virtual dismissal of any role for the bishops in governing the Church (the pope could do it alone) and by the council's giving Paul the opportunity by reaffirming papal supremacy. "The great weakness of Vatican II," he commented, "was that it compromised with Vatican I." He might well have said "surrendered to," but this was before his own compulsory invitation to taste the delights of harrassment by the papal establishment.

Within four or five years after the council's last session the Roman doctrinaires were back in the saddle, but there was some question as to whether there was a horse under it. By then, for example, Paul's encyclical flatly condemning contraception had been issued (in 1968), yet it seemed to be having about as much effect on Catholic behavior at the grass-roots level as the liquor-banning Volsted Act had on American behavior in the 1920s. The Church could be in danger, Schillebeeckx feared, of "becoming more and more a top without a base," and it would have to change. But "change," of course, is a naughty word, not to bandied about by pipsqueak doctors of divinity.

Indeed, in his book on marriage he argued that morality in that relationship depends on a recognition of human dignity rather than on some purpose of marital sex labeled "intrinsic" such as procreation. (The council's ferrets must have overlooked this statement before his assignment to help write that final draft on marriage, but apparently he was either circumspect or over-ruled, for the published version was safely orthodox.) He seems to have tended more and more to write or say provocative things during the late sixties and early seventies in his lectures and books on the council, collegiality, the role of the laity, clerical celibacy, and other nettlesome topics.

He was attracting Rome's attention. In July 1967, during an American lecture tour, he asserted that Christian revelation was being presented in outmoded terms, unsuited to a modern secular society and failing to offer "any valid answer to the questions about God asked by most people." In 1968 he refused a request, or order, that he introduce Paul's birth-control encyclical on a Dutch television program. And then in 1974 he published his first Jesus book with its neglect of the Chalcedonian amenities, followed three years later by his second Jesus book, and two years after that by his summons to Rome, inquisition, defense by Cardinal Willebrands, and orders to write more clearly in the future. And perhaps he did (write more clearly). At least there seemed to be no doubt that in his next book, on the Christian ministry (published in 1980), he came out against the requirement of clerical celibacy and for women in the priesthood. Such clarity Rome could do without.

In September 1982 Schillebeeckx retired from the university to read his books, write, and nurse his heart trouble. And, as he has put it, to "speak to God" as "a man speaks to a friend."

That same month he was awarded the national Erasmus Prize for Theology.

Charles E. Curran

"Pity Charlie Curran. There is hardly a better-liked priest among the whole body of Catholic theologians in the United States. He works hard, is conscientious, shows intellectual courage, and is open and friendly even with those with whom he is in disagreement. He has made many sacrifices in his life, including years of celibacy. Father Curran loves the Church." So spake the Catholic lay theologian Michael Novak in *The National Review* in April 1986, when the Roman doctrinaires were still only "questioning" Curran's opinions on sexual morality—on contraception, sterilization, abortion, masturbation, premarital intercourse, homosexual acts, the indissolubility of marriage—and, incidentally, euthanasia.

Curran is a professional celibate but an exceptional one. Any American who was subjected to Catholic education during the first half of this century can recall the relentless emphasis on sex provided by professional celibates in the classroom, both men and women. A student could readily emerge from their obsessive indoctrination with the impression that an "impure thought" was mortally sinful *per se,* but that the sinfulness of, say, lying or stealing depended on the circumstances. "Morality" meant sexual morality—*strict* sexual morality—unless otherwise noted. The pursed-lip set have been dominant in Roman Catholicism since the 1500s, when the Reformers revolted against the epidemic of cloistered dalliance, among other things, and swung the Catholic pendulum to its other, bluenosed extreme. The tension between compulsive asceticism and compulsive hedonism, with most of us caught in between, doubtless is as old as religion. But a difference between the two extremes is that dedicated ascetics usually are very much concerned with other people's sexual morality while dedicated hedonists generally couldn't care less. Jesus himself complained about busy-body accusations against his eating and drinking and consorting with sinners, the sinners being male taxgatherers and female you-know-whats.

The concern with others' sexual behavior has been a troubling element in Christianity from its beginnings, especially since around the year 400, when the ex-libertine doctor of morality, St. Augustine, placed his towering authority at the disposal of the sex-is-nasty school, which argued strongly that sex, although barely tolerable among the married laity, was wholly incompatible with the divinely ordained superiority of the clergy. Some eight centuries later this was the dominant school, supported by Roman authority if not exemplified in Roman conduct. With the onset of the Reformation the Council of Trent, to end the era of blatant hypocrisy, set clerical celibacy in concrete and mounted it on a pedestal for purposes of reverence.

Meanwhile St. Thomas Aquinas had lent *his* towering authority to the notion of "natural law," a moral law arising out of human nature, applicable to all mankind, and useful for writing moral prescriptions over and above the injunctions in the Bible. The sex-is-nasty advocates found this notion very useful indeed. Focusing on the genitals, they concluded that God had created sex for procreation; therefore any sexual activity conducted for any other reason frustrates his design and is morally wrong—"intrinsically" wrong, of its very nature. Since procreation naturally included raising children properly, and since God had instituted marriage for such long-term procreation, sexual activity outside marriage also was morally wrong. In the catechisms and theology manuals sex became a severe no-no, excepting dutifully pro-creative sex in marriage, and even this was treated with a kind of taciturn disdain, especially when it was unduly pleasurable by celibate standards. This seems to be essentially the position of John Paul & Co. today, despite occasional pious obeisances toward Vatican II. It is also the position to which Charles Curran takes notorious exception.

This application of natural law to sex, he argues, distorts the idea of natural law by limiting it to our animal nature, whereas Aquinas extended it to include our human, rational nature. Strict natural-law advocates have maintained, for instance, that lying is intrinsically wrong because God created speech for the communication of truth, and lying of its nature frustrates this purpose. But consider the classic case of someone sitting at the fork of a road who sees a child run fearfully down the north road and then sends a pursuing known child abuser down the south road. The misdirection may be intrinsically wrong for a computer designed to provide only the facts. But for a human being capable of thinking and seeing the implications of the situation? Curran would of course answer No. And so would most everyone else. This is not a surrender to "situation ethics." It is a recognition of human decisions as human, not mechanical.

Likewise in sex. Roman doctrinaires hold that masturbation is gravely sinful (assuming full knowledge and consent, whatever "full" means) because "spilling the seed" frustrates God's purpose. But this notion of the "seed" reaches back to a time long before the biology of procreation was understood, Curran contends, certainly before it was understood well enough to identify *the* divine purpose behind it. For many centuries the doctrinaires cited the punishment of Onan in the Book of Genesis for spilling his seed, until Biblical scholarship persuaded all but the hopelessly benighted that Onan's sin was his deliberate failure to provide his brother's widow with children according to Jewish law. But for the time being the vestigial notion of the procreative seed, a little human being (or "homunculus") seeking the comforts of the womb, with no recognition of the female ovarian contribution, seems practically ineradicable. The application of Rome's absolute prohibition to, say, adolescent masturbation—a prohibition hanging from a sky-hooked divination of God's purpose with no recognition of God-created psychological factors—according to Curran "distorts the meaning of human sexuality." In contrast with deductive rationalization based on divination, a more inductive approach "gives more importance to what other sciences tell us about man and his actions."

In general Curran believes that "masturbation is wrong since it fails to integrate sexuality into the service of love." But usually not "gravely" wrong nor "mortally sinful": "Individual masturbatory actions are not that important provided there is general enough growth toward communion with others and interpersonal relationships."

Likewise he believes "that homosexual actions are wrong. Sexuality seems to have its meaning in terms of a life-giving love union of male and female." But he shies away from labeling them as necessarily mortally sinful. The homosexual should be offered (and presumably should accept) help to extricate her/ him from her/his predicament. Yet when the effort proves futile, when the homosexuality is irreversible, homosexual acts might be the only way to achieve "some degree of humanity and stability." What he seems to be saying is that homosexuality is not simply uninhibited sodomy but can involve two persons in a genuine, enduring love relationship. If the only practical options are an impersonal homosexual promiscuity and a caring homosexual fidelity, surely the latter is preferable. Since homosexuality often results from the sins of others who deprive children of the love they need and deserve, "the theology of compromise . . . seems most appropriate in these cases." But not, of course, to the uncompromising.

The theology of compromise may also be relevant, he believes, in some instances of sex before marriage. Having recalled that "Thomas admits that passion in sexual matters is very strong and difficult to overcome" (more so for some individuals than for others), Curran can see "quite limited . . . occasions where sexual intercourse outside marriage would not be wrong." But he concedes this warily: "The union of bodies is a lie and a false sign unless it bespeaks a total union of two hearts." Is either partner taking advantage of the other? Are both sufficiently aware of consequences, of the fact that in highly emotional situations like "war and sex there is always the danger of escalation"?

Compromise also enters into evaluating the practice of using contraceptives in premarital sex. While disapproving of casual, impersonal sex, which "violates the human meaning of sexuality . . . I and many others would urge people engaging in such sexual intercourse to use contraception as a way of avoiding conception. Such people obviously are not prepared to bring children into the world and educate them." The use of the word "urge" in this context must have been gleefully reported to the Vatican watchdogs by many a Mrs. Grundy addicted to watching hackles rise.

Then what of the practice of using contraceptives in marital sex? Curran cites a survey statistic, offered by the president of the National Conference of Catholic Bishops, to the effect that over 70% of Catholic married couples in the U.S. in the 1980s are limiting births through means condemned by Paul VI in his apodictic encyclical and by John Paul in speech after speech after speech. This obviously says something about laypeople's attitude toward papal authority and may even suggest a problem for consideration at headquarters, however hard the head. But Rome has spoken, so the case is closed.

Or is it? It was opened a crack in the early 1950s, when Pius XII gave grudging sanction to the rhythm method of birth control requiring continence during periods of ovulation but otherwise allowing intercourse for reasons other than procreation (so long as no artificial means were introduced to prevent untimely conception). While former popes spun in their graves, this opinion became a kind of Catholic sexual shibboleth until the conjunction of Paul's encyclical and the introduction of new, more effective and more convenient means of artificial birth control (such as the pill) thrust "natural family planning" into the background.

Curran finds much to be said for natural family planning. It is physically natural, avoiding additives, pills, devices. It is physically safe—no cancer, liver disease, phlebitis, uterine bleeding or other side-effects occasionally associated with contraceptive practices. It calls for a higher order of human behavior in self-control, and it makes its demands on both partners rather than only the woman. Nevertheless he believes, together with the vast majority of his fellow citizens, that it "does not appear to be effective where discipline, training, and high motivation-are not present." Given the emotional needs of most married couples and the pressing problems of population growth, he believes, again with the vast majority of his fellow citizens, that artificial contraception offers personal and social benefits that outweigh the slight health risk and debatable moral considerations. "There do seem to be many attractive aspects about natural family planning, but I personally see no moral problem in using other forms of contraception as a means of exercising responsible parenthood." That spinning noise this time is St. Augustine.

It is hardly surprising that the doctrinaires' opinion on sterilization likewise sits in concrete: "Sterilization," intone the directives for Catholic health facilities, "whether permanent or temporary, for man or for woman, may not be used as a means of contraception." And it is equally unsurprising that Curran again dissents, since, as he has pointed out, the moral issues are basically the same, the only difference being that the likely permanent effect of sterilization requires "a more permanent or serious reason to justify it." Nor need it be justified only for medical reasons; there can be important "sociological, psychological, economic or other" reasons as well.

Another Augustine-rotating feature of modern technology is artificial insemination of a wife by her husband or, if he is sterile, by a "donor." In either case it has been papally condemned because the semen is obtained by masturbation, which, being intrinsically evil, may not be used as a means to any end. In the "donor" case there is the additional objection of adultery. In his condemnation Pius XII uncharacteristically but unavoidably swung the focus from procreation to that "secondary purpose" of expressing love: "Artificial insemination is condemned precisely because it separates procreation from the personal act of loving self-surrender."

Curran respectfully disagrees. Not every single sex act must be physically expressive of the love union; that union consists of, and is expressed in, the durable loving relationship between the marriage partners. "Consequently, with many other Catholic theologians I accept the morality of artificial insemination by the husband." Also like many other Catholic theologians, he is much less confident about the morality of insemination by donor: "I cannot exclude the possibility that [such insemination] could be a morally good choice in some circumstances despite serious problems that are present." On the question of such insemination outside marriage, he is downright dogmatic: given the Judaeo-Christian tradition of child-rearing in marriage, it "is morally unacceptable."

His position on *in vitro* fertilization, which brings sperm and egg together outside the womb (for later implantation therein) forms something of a bridge to his position on abortion. That which applies to artificial insemination similarly applies to the *in vitro* method except that the latter involves the likelihood of discarding embryos during the sometimes difficult process of implantation. Roman doctrinaires, arbitrarily holding that embryos are human beings and not to be discarded, condemn the method as absolutely immoral. Curran cannot see these collections of cells as truly human individuals and therefore cannot accept that discarding them is murder. Although they "do have a value and importance . . . some discards and failures cannot constitute an absolute condemnation of *in vitro* fertilization and embryo transplant." Their loss is justified by the method's success, when the result is, at least eventually, an undeniable human being.

As for abortion, he similarly cannot accept that it is murder, maintaining as he does that "truly individual human life is not present until two or three weeks after conception [although] before this time the zygote, morula, and blastocyst do have some value and importance." For him, the emphasis in this statement is on "individual." And so his view is much different regarding later stages of pregnancy: he "cannot accept the solution of abortion of deformed fetuses, since a truly individual human life is already present." He accepts the U.S. Supreme Court's famous decision and is against the efforts to overturn it through a Constitutional amendment. "In our pluralistic society, in which there is a dispute about the beginning of human life, I can understand a conclusion which says that the benefit of the doubt should be given to the rights of the mother and her freedom to act."

Another feature of our pluralistic society is the popularity of divorce and remarriage. Traditionally Rome has held that *any* marriage freely entered into and physically consummated is indissoluble of its very nature, although recently, Curran observes, it has held a contradictory view that the pope has the power to dissolve marriages involving unbaptized persons. For the hapless baptized, however, marriage is forever. Catholics who divorce and remarry are excommunicated, ultimately because of Jesus' assertion that remarriage equals adultery. But scholarly study of the relevant passages in the New Testament (e.g., Mk 10:11 and Lk 16:18, as well as 1 Cor 7) has raised questions about their applying to cases arising twenty centuries later in a totally different milieu, especially one in which Christians no longer expect the imminent end of all marriage in a looming Armageddon. Sociological study suggests that first marriages can be disastrous mistakes and second marriages great successes even by conventional Christian standards, so much so that various ways of getting around Rome's rigidity are being followed quite generally at the pastoral level. Given the strong inductive evidence against the doctrinaires' deductive logic, Curran has concluded "that the Roman Catholic Church should change its teaching and practice on divorce." Indissolubility is a goal to strive for through mutual love, attainable but not by everyone. People differ, temperaments differ, circumstances differ, marriages differ. And they all are subject to change. Nothing so variable should be *required* to be forever.

What is *not* subject to change is the opinion of John Paul & Co., as Rome has made abundantly clear. Any recommendation for change is thus unworthy of a Catholic theologian—a *truly* Catholic theologian.

An exception may be euthanasia—a subject extraordinarily removed from Rome's endemic obsession with the indisputability of its authority and with other people's sexual conduct. The doctrinaires' position is that no human life may be deliberately ended (except in self-defense and invigorating enterprises like war and crusades). Life must be sustained by ordinary means but not necessarily by extraordinary means. Curran agrees with the principle but finds it hard to apply in practice, with modern technology blurring the distinction between ordinary and extraordinary means. "The matter is so complex that the present teaching as proposed by the authoritative, noninfallible magisterium cannot claim and, to its credit, does not claim to exclude the possibility of error."

That phrase, "noninfallible magisterium," is an important one for Curran. Like many other theologians, he does not know of a matter of morals (as distinct from a doctrine of faith) on which Rome has issued an infallible declaration, so identified. A noninfallible assertion, he maintains, is by definition open to question. For this opinion, and for his consequent dissent from the party line on sexual morality, in the late summer of 1986 he was declared a Catholic non-theologian.

* * *

Charles E. Curran was born in March 1934 in Rochester, New York, where he attended St. Bernard's Seminary and College. He spent most of his twenties in Rome, where, in 1961, he received his doctorate in theology from the Gregorian University and the Academia Alphonsiana. Having been ordained a priest in 1958, he returned from Rome in 1961 to teach moral theology at St. Bernard's. In 1965 he was hired by the Catholic University of

America to teach moral theology as assistant professor (1965-67), then associate professor (1967-71) and full professor. He has been president of the American Society of Christian Ethics (1971-72) and vice-president and president of the Catholic Theological Society of America (1968-69, 1969-70). He has written abundantly on theological subjects, some would say too abundantly, at least for his own good.

In April 1967 he was summarily fired. The university pooh-bahs, being papally oriented, gave no reason for his dismissal, but there was little doubt that his unorthodox views on birth control (which he had *expressed!*) had pursed many an administrative lip. Although mild-mannered, Curran is gifted with a generous dollop of stubborn courage. He decided to resist. A popular teacher, he had the support of his students and, more effectively, that of his colleagues on the faculty, who voted 400 to 18 to discontinue classes until he was reinstated. The boycott lasted for three days, closing down the university and bringing the administration to its senses. Not only was Curran rehired, but it also was announced that he would be promoted to associate professor in the fall.

By the late summer of 1968 he was in hot water again. For several months he and others had been troubled by reports that Paul VI, who had appointed a commission to study Catholic teaching on birth control, was on the verge of issuing an encyclical which, contrary to the commission's strong recommendation, would in effect simply reiterate his revered predecessors' flat condemnation of all artificial birth-control methods. By summer they felt quite sure he would do so, thereby alienating not only most non-Catholic Christians and non-Christians but also an untold number of Catholics, especially Catholic couples. Perhaps, they felt, a public statement from Catholic theologians, immediately following the encyclical and offering respectful dissent, would soften the shock and reduce the alienation. By late July the mass media were reporting that the disastrous encyclical was imminent. With such advance warning, American Catholic theologians could hardly be unprepared.

The encyclical was issued on July 29, but *Time* had obtained a copy the day before for a detailed report on the morning of the 29th. That afternoon a group of Catholic University professors, with Curran in the vanguard, met with some other theologians and agreed on the statement to be released on the 30th at a press conference already scheduled for another purpose. During a long night at the telephones, reading the statement to other theologians, they obtained public endorsements from 87 of their scholarly colleagues. At the press conference the next day about ten of the signers were present to explain that this was not rebellion but interpretation. Nevertheless it created quite a stir.

After respectfully acknowledging "a distinct role of hierarchical *magisterium* (teaching authority) in the Church," the statement asserted theologians' traditional responsibility to interpret and evaluate that authority's pronouncements. The encyclical, it pointed out, was not infallible and was therefore subject to responsible dissent and correction. "Past authoritative statements on religious liberty, interest-taking, the right to silence, and the end of marriage have all been corrected at a later date." The encyclical tended to equate the hierarchy with the Church as a whole, relied on a narrow view of papal authority, depended on an inadequate concept of natural law, overstressed the physical aspects of sex, and merely echoed previous teaching. Then came the statement's clincher, guaranteed to lift doctrinaire temperatures to the boiling point: "Therefore, as Roman Catholic theologians, conscious of our duty and our limitations, we conclude that spouses may responsibly decide according to their conscience that artificial contraception in some circumstances is permissible and indeed necessary to preserve and foster the values and sacredness of marriage." This would appear in the press, some "scandal"-sensitive doctrinaires warned—and some of the faithful can *read*! And misinform others!

The next day, the 31st, letters went out to some 1200 members of the Catholic Theological Society of America (Charles Curran, vice-president) and the College Theology Society, inviting their approval of the statement. Eventually more than 600 recipients, with credentials in theology, philosophy, canon law and other pertinent disciplines, came out with public endorsements. The National Conference of Catholic Bishops, however, stuck loyally, or obsequiously, by the pope; Rome has spoken, the case is closed.

Meanwhile, back at the University, Curran and nineteen of his colleagues found themselves on the receiving end of uncomprehending stares and disapproving frowns. The university's Chancellor O'Boyle was also Washington's archbishop, in a position to deliver a double whammy, and he had publicly proscribed any dissent in his diocese. In medieval Europe he might simply have excommunicated the dissident twenty and turned them over to a cooperative civil government for toasting, but in pluralistic modern American he decided, after some inconclusive meetings, to turn the matter over to the university's board of trustees, which promptly turned it over to a board of inquiry, which in turn held hearings and meetings over five months between October 1968 and April 1969. In April the board of inquiry reported to the university's Academic Senate, which unanimously accepted the report. In it the board exonerated the professors, reprimanded the trustees for threatening to suspend them, and urged the administration to adopt some measure of academic freedom and due process. It was so favorable to the professors that some apoplectic doctrinaires charged that it had merely echoed their opinions. Doctrinaires are, of course, experts on echoing.

This outcome must have stuck painfully in the Roman craw, and Curran, as principal organizer and spokesman for the chorus of dissent, must have made it to the enemies' list swiftly and securely. But personnel changes in Rome delayed action in this witch-hunt as in many others. It would be many years before Rome could turn again to the Curran chase. Meanwhile he had been teaching and writing in the same old vein, especially on that nasty subject, sex. And the Congregation for the Doctrine of the Faith had been urging him to "reconsider and retract those positions which violate the conditions for a professor to be called a Catholic theologian." It is a contradiction, advised a September 1985 letter from Cardinal Joseph Ratzinger, head of the CDF, when "one who is to teach in the name of the church in fact denies her teaching." The affectionate "her" referred to John Paul & Co.; i.e., *Our*.

After several frustrating exchanges by mail, with Ratzinger demanding indications of conformity and Curran asking what kind of conformity, in a correspondence reverberating with more questions than answers, the two men met in Rome in March 1986. Their exchange solved nothing. Curran afterward told reporters simply that his views on sexual ethics were deemed unacceptable. Thus his dismissal from the university seemed inevitable, as well as his being branded as a Catholic non-theologian.

Although American Catholic hardheads, such as the Catholics United for the Faith, doubtless found this news mouthwatering, it aroused considerable protest from others. The nine former presidents of the Catholic Theological Society of America, agreeing with Curran that his views represented those of most Catholic theologians, circulated a petition in his behalf. Cardinal Bernadin of Chicago tried to get John Paul and Ratzinger to accept Curran's compromise offer not to teach classes in sexual ethics, in vain of course. Perhaps the most eloquent support came from Matthew Clark, bishop of Curran's home town of Rochester. After praising Curran as priest and scholar, he commented:

> It is, I believe, commonly accepted in the Roman Catholic theological community that Father Curran is a moral theologian of notable competence whose work locates him very much at the center of that community and not at all on the fringe. I believe that perception is true. If Father Curran's status as a Roman Catholic theologian is brought into question, I fear a serious setback to Catholic education and pastoral life in this country. That could happen in two ways. Theologians may stop exploring the challenging questions of the day in a creative, healthy way because they fear actions which may prematurely end their teaching careers. Moreover, able theologians may abandon Catholic institutions altogether in order to avoid embarrassing confrontation with Church authorities. Circumstances of this sort would seriously undermine the standing of Catholic scholarship in this nation, isolate our theological community, and weaken our Catholic institutions of higher education.

CHARLES E. CURRAN

In August 1986, as succinctly reported the following October in *Time* (under the heading, "John Paul's Cleanup Campaign"), Rome and its American minions "ended Father Charles Curran's career at the Catholic University of America, citing his open disagreements with Catholic moral teachings on birth control and other issues." The mills of the university gods, however, ground the issues slowly and exceedingly fine. About twenty months later the "end" turned out to have been a suspension subject to review by a university committee. This review concluded that Curran's right to tenure should be respected, whereupon the trustees announced that, although he could not belong to the faculty of the graduate theology school chartered by Rome, he could teach elsewhere at the university in an "area of his professional competence."

If they could find one, presumably.

The Liberation Theologians

If there is anything nastier than sex in the Roman glossary, it surely must be Marxism. For John Paul, Marxism is "the anti-Church . . . the anti-Gospel"—his "great Satan," to borrow an epithet from another eminent religious leader. To Roman doctrinaires, despite cardinals' fondness for the color, it is the Red Menace. Its infernal glow lends to other social philosophies a pink, or pinko, coloration which makes the doctrinaires see red. And that, in general, seems to be the story of John Paul & Co. and liberation theology, at least for the time being.

About a quarter of a century ago liberation theology arose in Latin America chiefly as a response to the "base communities" being formed in thousands of villages through the cooperation of the peasant laity and socially conscious clergy. These small, local groups—there may be as many as a quarter million of them today—meet every few days for group prayer, Bible study, and discussion of common social and political problems (building a health center, forming a labor union or political committee).

They naturally have encountered various degrees of resistance from political, economic and ecclesiastical power blocs, for they are inspired by the desperate need to narrow the notorious gap between the rich and the poor, between the powerful and the powerless, throughout Central and South America. (Although they don't cite it, they could well be inspired by the Lord's request in Isaiah 58:6, "The kind of fasting I want is this: remove the chains of oppression and the yoke of injustice, and let the oppressed go free.")

Even John Paul, whose exalted position allows him to travel piously about the world in a comfortably furnished private plane and to have a swimming pool installed in his summer place, has described this endemic social injustice as "horrifying," as an "intolerable abyss." Thus the pope and the mavericks in this controversy agree that the abyss is intolerable. But the mavericks feel the Church's hierarchy and clergy should *do* something about the situation, whereas the pope keeps telling them to keep out of it, to leave it to the laity. He is also very skittish about the Marxist strain in the mavericks' social philosophy.

GUSTAVO GUTIÉRREZ

He has reason to be. Much of their writing has the flavor of the *Communist Manifesto,* with emphasis on the class struggle between the exploiters and the exploited. Other maverick theologians generally try to introduce a note of uncertainty into their discussions, protesting against the absolute certitude claimed and demanded by Roman dogmatists. Not the liberation theologians; their ideological cast of mind generally produces dicta as absolute as Rome's, although not so often divorced from common sense. They are not addicted to the subjunctive mood.

A sample: "To participate in class struggle not only is not opposed to universal love; this commitment is today the necessary and inescapable means of making this love concrete. For this participation is what leads to a classless society without owners and dispossessed, without oppressors and oppressed." Rome has no monopoly on deductive thinking. (History, said Henry Ford, is bunk.)

This aggressively dogmatic assertion appears in a book written in the early 1970s by a mild, affable, unassuming Peruvian priest, Gustavo Gutiérrez. If anyone can be called the father of liberation theology, it is surely he; and if any book can be called the seminal book of liberation theology, it is surely his *A Theology of Liberation*. After his exposure to what he calls "the dominant theology" in Europe, including a semester at the Vatican's Gregorian University, he returned to Peru only to find this theology, with its dedication to personal salvation and its neglect of social injustice, totally inadequate in his pastoral work among people in desperate need of food, shelter, health care and human respect. If the gospel was to mean anything to these people, he decided, it would have to offer them liberation not only from their own sins but also from the sins of others, liberation not simply from their misery but rather from the social-economic-political systems that oppressed them. "The fact that these people are poor and not rich is not just a matter of chance, but the result of a structure," and that structure would have to be dismantled. And so, in effect, would the church's hierarchical establishment that had been so much a part of that structure ever since the Christian gentlemen arrived from Spain and Portugal to brutalize the native Americans.

And how is the dismantling to be done against the resistance of the vested interests? Here he has had the challenging problem of treading on eggs without being accused of pussyfooting. He has solved it ingeniously by appealing to an historical truth that has never received the attention it deserves. Violence, he maintains, already exists in an oppressive society, but passively, as a constant threat, becoming active only when needed to maintain (or restore) "law and order." To put it in a North American context, he would surely identify as a victim of violence an employee fired for refusing to mow the boss's lawn or share the boss's bed. Just how physical and active an establishment's violence can become has been abundantly demonstrated during the racial turmoil a quarter of a century ago in the post-Confederate South and more lately in South Africa. Establishment violence, because it is so widespread and enduring, is much worse than any brief violence that may accompany efforts to dismantle the oppressive social structure.

And how does this tally with the gospel's demand that we love our enemies? The oppressors are the enemies, Gutiérrez answers, but displacing them and punishing them is really loving them, liberating them from an evil social structure and "from themselves." Here he might have been more persuasive by recalling the gospel's demand that we love others as ourselves—and our oppressive enemies less than our oppressed parents, our oppressed children and our oppressed neighbors.

Oppression, however, is not all that deplorable among Roman doctrinaires. It is, indeed, rather their stock in trade. Catholicism is for everyone; it must not, they insist, exclude these so-called oppressors, without whose generous support the Church itself would be poor. (For "Church" read "Hierarchy.") Exactly, replies Gutiérrez, the Church *should* be a Church of the poor, should display "a preferential option for the poor." The poor must be liberated from chronic oppression, he argues, and (hauling out the red flag for the doctrinaire *toros*), "socialism, moreover, represents the most fruitful and far-reaching approach" for liberating them in "a society in which private ownership of the means of production is eliminated." As for the Church, its unity is "a myth which must disappear if the Church is to be 'reconverted' to the service of the workers in the class struggle."

The pungent odor of Marxism eventually found its way to sensitive noses in the Vatican. In September 1984 the Congregation for the Doctrine of the Faith issued an "Instruction on Certain Aspects of the 'Theology of Liberation,'" signed by Cardinal Ratzinger, for distribution among bishops and others needing divine guidance. It conceded that social justice in Latin America was probably less than ideal. "In certain parts" of the region, "the seizure of the vast majority of the wealth by an oligarchy of owners bereft of social consciousness, the practical absence of a rule of law, military dictators making a mockery of elementary human rights, the corruption of certain powerful officials, the savage practices of some foreign capital interests"—all encourage revolt among people who "consider themselves" the victims. A deplorable situation, perhaps, but certain things must *not* be done, or even thought, about it. Liberation theology can lead to "a perversion of the Christian message as God entrusted it to his Church." (For "Church" read "Rome.") It tends to confuse the kingdom of God with social liberation through class struggle, and the church of the people with a church of the oppressed; to oppose the hierarchy as representatives of the oppressors; and to neglect the sacraments, especially the Real Presence in the Eucharist.

Whether these tendencies existed in all liberation theologies, whether this was an accurate characterization of liberation theology in general, was not the point. The point was that a solution of social injustices lies not in social action but "only by making an appeal to the moral potential of the person" and by "interior conversion." Those rights-mocking dictators, for example, presumably needed only a little gentle proselytizing to make everything all right. Violence is self-defeating, counseled the instruction, despite the tradition which Rome established during the Crusades, when a much more precious ox was being gored.

It has been suggested that the instruction may not have been issued with John Paul's full approval, but anyone who believes that will also believe that Russia was invaded over Napoleon's and Hitler's protests. Indeed, in 1986 the pope himself underlined the instruction's counsel of much talk and little do when he taped a televised message to Brazilian Catholics that merely decried hunger and poverty. Earlier that year, when the Philippines' Cardinal Jaime Sim publicly recommended that Ferdinand Marcos relinquish the presidency that he had "obtained by fraud" in a notoriously fraudulent snap election, the cardinal was summoned to Rome to be given a papal reprimand for such outrageous political activity.

John Paul is thought to have had more to do with a second, related pronouncement issued in April 1986, an "Instruction on Christian Freedom and Liberation," which waffled adroitly enough to be hailed as vindication by liberation theologians *and* their conservative critics. It praised the idea of base communities *if* they were subject to the local bishops. While declaring Catholic social teaching open to new ideas, it stressed that the condemnation of "tendencies" in the previous instruction "appear ever more timely and relevant." While deploring establishment violence, it relegated counter-violence to last-resort status, proposing non-violent resistance as "having no less prospects for success." John Paul summed it up for the bishops of Brazil when he described liberation theology to them as "not only orthodox but necessary" *if* "purified of elements that can adulterate it."

*   *   *

Gustavo Gutiérrez was born in Lima, Peru, in June 1928. After studying medicine and then philosophy at local universities, he traveled to Belgium, where he earned a master's degree in philosophy and psychology at the Catholic University in Louvain in 1955. Four years later, having changed course again and now armed with a degree in theology from Lyon in France, he was ordained a priest and moved to Rome for a semester at the Gregorian University. It would be twenty years more before he received his doctorate in theology, an honorary degree from the University of Nijmegen in The Netherlands.

Meanwhile he had returned to Lima to join the Catholic Pontifical University's Department of Theology and Social Sciences and to act as counselor for the National Union of Catholic Students, as well as for a number of prayer and discussion groups in the city. In 1968 he was appointed theological advisor to the

Second Conference of Latin American Bishops at Medellin, Colombia. In that year also he attended a conference in Peru of radically oriented priests, whom he had helped to organize into the formidably titled National Office of Investigation. Their consensus was that mankind cannot live by theology alone; bread is a prerequisite, and so is human dignity. The "dominant" theology of the seminaries, very Thomist and very Roman, heavily committed to achieving one's own salvation after a trip through a divinely ordained vale of tears, was too tolerant of the social injustice largely responsible for the tears. The people, trying to gain some measure of freedom from the tyranny of landowners, employers and associated bishops, were forming into local groups, called "base communities," for grass-roots religious and social activities. They needed a theology related to solving their overriding problem.

And so Gutiérrez provided it, or at least an expression of it, in his book, *A Theology of Liberation*. Published in Peru in 1971, it soon appeared in several languages and began earning him a reputation. Invitations to speak came from both Americas, Europe, Asia, Africa. His speaking and further writing enhanced his reputation, which eventually attracted Rome's attention, automatically stimulating anathema impulses.

Early in 1983 John Paul & Co., with Ratzinger providing the spearhead, dispatched a cautionary critique of Gutiérrez's writings to a conference of Peruvian bishops. A decision was expected of them: this upstart priest and his upstart liberation theologians must be squelched. But Rome seemed unaware that the Latin American bishops were undergoing a change of heart. Only about a third of those at the conference were establishment lovers. Another third supported liberation theology in general, and the rest hovered in between. As a result, the bishops' response was not nearly obsequious enough to suit Vatican tastes.

It took the form of two reports issued in the summer of 1984. The majority report censured him, the minority report supported him. Rome, allegedly complaining that the bishops were incompetent to handle the matter properly, and being anxious that the majority report might suffer in comparison with the minority report (drafted by more reputable if not abler theologians), opted for accepting neither report. Instead, all 52 Peruvian bishops were ordered to Rome for realignment, and 45 were able to make the trip. They were subjected to several meetings with Ratzinger and John Paul, in which they began to sense that the two men were not entirely of the same mind on the matter. The cardinal wanted obedient censure of the mavericks while the pope seemed less demanding, more sympathetic with the bishops' uneasiness over the economic criminality of concentrated wealth amid widespread privation.

After their return to Peru the bishops issued a third report, this time a single one which neither supported nor condemned the upstart priest. Thus he apparently was saved by people who had the courage of their convictions, and by people who did not.

LEONARDO BOFF

The Peruvian lack of servility may have triggered some sober second thinking on the part of John Paul & Co. concerning liberation theology, at least at the level of tactics. In 1981, ten years after the appearance of *A Theology of Liberation,* a Brazilian Franciscan priest named Leonardo Boff published *Church: Charism and Power,* with the explanatory subtitle, *Liberation Theology and the Institutional Church.* In its pages liberation theology wound up smelling much nicer than the institutional Church. But when the Roman doctrinaires condemned the book, nary a word was said about liberation theology. The hot potato apparently was to be set aside to let it cool off a bit.

The book's central thesis pictured the Catholic Church as undergoing a fundamental change. The Church of power, the institution reaching back to the Emperor Constantine, is beginning a metamorphosis into a Church of charism, or of charisms, in which all its members exercise their God-given and God-centered talents (their "charisms") in the service of God and neighbor— democratically, equally, without rank and its privileges. This is the way it is done in the burgeoning base communities, and this is the way the Church must go. No more dictatorial shepherds, no more subservient sheep.

In illustration, Boff quoted a couple of popes. "The rigid separation between clergy and laity was emphasized by Gregory XVI (1831-46): 'No one can deny that the Church is an unequal society in which God destined some to be governors and others to be servants. The latter are the laity; the former, the clergy.' Pius X is even more rigid: 'Only the college of pastors have the right and authority to lead and govern. The masses have no right or authority except that of being governed, like an obedient flock that follows its Shepherd.' " This type of relationship Boff described as a pathological one "which dehumanizes both parties." It is small wonder that in Latin America, with its dictatorial regimes, "this model of the Church tends to predominate." But in the Church of charism, faith "is the faith of the entire Church and not only that of the hierarchy."

Such faith cannot be confined in an ivory tower. It must relate to the real world, the contemporary world in which social injustice cries for remedy. The theology of liberation "begins with indignation at the poverty experienced by God's children, a poverty that God surely does not will." This leads to a series of steps to liberate them, and thus "Christian faith lends its specific contribution to this global process of liberation by pointing out nonviolent means, the strength of love, the inexhaustible capacity of dialogue and persuasion as well as by helping to understand the sometimes unavoidable violence toward those who block any change whatsoever." The "as well as" phrase is significant, of course, since "sometimes" probably means at least "usually."

The individual Christian must do her/his duty. Since "no desire is efficacious without organization," the liberation movement must have "organizing centers and offices such as those for legal defense, human rights, justice and peace, and so forth. The Christian must join in the work of these centers as well as participate in unions and neighborhood organizations, thereby joining others in the struggle for justice." The charism of the contemplative life is not mentioned. The word "must" has a peculiar ring in a context of protest against regimentation, but, as was mentioned earlier, liberation theology is not conspicuously riven by doubt. The new regimentation will not come from "above," for the "the laity do not need the backing of their bishop or pastor for their movement to have a 'Christian character,' " as the Latin American bishops meeting at Puebla had conceded.

The chapter labeled "The Violation of Human Rights in

the Church" was not designed to earn approving smiles from Roman countenances. It protested the practice of selecting official leadership only by appointment from on high, denounced the callous treatment of actual and would-be ex-priests, excoriated the relegation of women to second-class membership (ridiculing the Congregation's assertion that females can't be ordained because Jesus was male), and deplored the secrecy and "psychological torture" associated with the "Kafkaesque" inquisition procedures. In this connection Boff offered a novel, somewhat Marxian and quite perceptive view of the Church as a society in which "one group produces the symbolic goods and another consumes them." The first group, by selectively withholding the spiritually nourishing goods, can and does control the second most effectively; even emperors have succumbed. The authority of the Church, he added, is not in question, but rather the way it has been and is being exercised.

Rome's arbitrary exercise of power stems from what Boff calls the "paganization of Christianity" through its recognition by the Roman emperors in the fourth century and from the assertion of papal power by Gregory VII in the eleventh. The Church took on the ruler-subject coloration of its secular environment, holding to it long after that environment had radically changed. With the Reformation, "Catholicism became a total, reactionary, violent, and repressive ideology." As in "any other totalitarian power," reason is expected to serve the system, whose perpetuation is ever the paramount objective. Thus Rome will tolerate "authoritarian and even totalitarian regimes as long as its own rights are not attacked." In the 1930s Pius XI decided that, in Spain, the Franco insurrection against that pinko republican government was a justifiable use of violence to establish a Church-respecting dictatorship, which thereafter became Rome's great comfort.

All this is changing, the book asserted, in a process of "ecclesiogenesis." A new Church is being born in the Christian base communities, a decentralized Church of the poor in which bishops, priests, religious and laity cooperate in making the faith more meaningful in today's world. Rome will call it disloyal, for indeed its development relies on "the continuing destruction of the notion of the Church issuing forth complete and fully formed from the Savior's hands." It is less exclusive: the Church of Christ "may also be present (subsist) in other Christian churches." It is not only a teaching Church but a learning Church as well, with everyone participating in both functions. It resembles the Church as it existed before Constantine, before its corruption by Roman imperialism. It restores Catholicism to the Catholic people.

The response of John Paul & Co. came in the form of a "notification" issued by the Congregation for the Doctrine of the Faith in March 1985. Without mentioning liberation theology, it declared that "the options of L. Boff analyzed here endanger the sound doctrine of the faith, which this Congregation has the task of promoting and safeguarding." The danger lay particularly in four areas: "the structure of the Church, the concept of dogma, the exercise of sacred power and the prophetic role."

As for Church structure, he was guilty of an "ecclesiological relativism" leading to "radical criticisms directed at the hierarchic structure of the Catholic Church." The relativism lay in his including other Christian denominations in the Church of Christ; actually, that Church is the Catholic Church, which others may merely resemble in some respects. Relativism also accounted for his proposal that dogma may change with the times, whereas actually "the sense of the dogmatic formulas always remains true and coherent, determined and unalterable, although it may be further clarified and better understood." ("Dogma" was not defined.) His charges against the exercise of sacred power—the withholding of sacramental product to control the consumers—reduces sacred functions to mere economics and "is equivalent to subverting religious reality" (also not defined). Finally, the prophetic role in the Church, although exercised by both hierarchy and laity, "must accept the hierarchy and the institutions," and the last word must be the hierarchy's. As in this instance.

*   *   *

Born in Brazil in 1938, Leonardo Boff received his education in theology in his native land and in Munich, Germany. Besides teaching theology in Petropolis, just north of Rio de Janeiro, and working with the poor, he has served as advisor to Brazil's Conference of Bishops and to the Latin American Conference of Religions. He has written several books, both before and after *Church: Charism and Power,* occasionally in collaboration with his brother Clodovis, a Servite priest and also a theologian and social worker, although one who has yet to be given the gimlet eye.

Leonardo completed his doctoral dissertation in Munich under the aegis of a fellow Franciscan improbably named Bonaventura Kloppenburg. At the time the archbishop of Munich was none other than the mavericks' nemesis-to-be, Cardinal Joseph Ratzinger. When the dissertation appeared in summary as Chapter 12 in *Church,* Kloppenburg, who had meanwhile turned into a dedicated adversary of liberation theology, wrote a detailed critique condemning the book as heretical. Boff sent a copy of the book and of the review to Ratzinger with a request for advice. The cardinal, who as archbishop had had a supervisory connection with the dissertation but was not head of the doctrinal Congregation, doubtless was too busy to read the lengthy critique much less the book, and he responded by simply suggesting that Boff publish a reply. Boff did so, and that seemed to end the matter.

But not long thereafter the book was brought to the dour attention of the Rio office of the Congregation, and in May 1984 he received a letter from Ratzinger accusing him of distorting traditional doctrines to fit new contexts, of implying that Jesus did not found the Church as presently constituted, of carelessness in discussing the role of dogma and scripture in preserving the faith, and of being contentious and impudent in treating the exercise of power in the Church. Hie yourself to Rome, he was told, and give an account of yourself.

He did so in September. With him as his defending theologian was the head of the Brazilian hierarchy, Cardinal Alois Lorscheider. Doubtless this helped to make the inquisitorial session less unpleasant, but the bureaucracy plodded on thereafter. In May 1985 John Paul & Co. ordered Boff to refrain from all publishing and lecturing activities until further notice. Boff obeyed, presumably happy to devote himself to his pastoral work. Later the ban was eased to permit him to teach classes and preach sermons. It lasted less than a year. The end coincided with the appearance in April 1986 of the aforementioned fence-straddling "Instruction on Christian Freedom and Liberation." It is hard to believe that the coincidence was merely a coincidence.

*   *   *

There are many other liberation theologians, but they have yet to feel the hot breath of John Paul & Co. The liberation movement is young, however, and Rome has quite a reputation for keeping meticulous dossiers. It is also famous for slow motion, and the pot may well boil over before the CDF can clamp on the lid.

Among those other liberal theologians is Juan Luis Segundo, who in 1985 responded to the "Instruction on Certain Aspects of the 'Theology of Liberation' " with a book entitled *Theology and the Church: A Response to Cardinal Ratzinger and a Warning to the Whole Church.* It was technical, often obsure and somewhat ambiguous, but it clearly and severely criticized the Instruction for its "negative evaluation of Vatican II and of the postconciliar period." Segundo's dossier may be accumulating data for an inquisition in the 1990s.

Raymond Hunthausen

The papal bureaucracy controls the appointment of bishops more securely that it does the emergence of theologians. It rarely goofs in making safe appointments, but every so often it lets someone slip by who can change with time and circumstances. It seems to have let an unconscionable number slip by in the case of the current Latin American bishops, many of whom have presented a united, and thus far insurmountable, bulwark against Roman interference in favor of the status quo. In this case Rome has been stymied by unity, but the far more usual case is that of the individual maverick bishop, in which cases it has more success. A stray is easier to round up than a stampede. Easier to brand, too. Usually.

The standing operating procedure in such cases is for Rome to send an "apostolic visitor" to spend some time in the suspect diocese, usually after receiving a spate of heated complaints about some goings-on or other. (There are groups of Catholics, especially of the neanderthal variety, who dedicate themselves to organizing letters-to-the-Vatican campaigns, confident of the bureaucracy's predisposition to treasure such see-and-tell reports.) In the spring of 1983, for instance, complaints were received (reportedly, allegedly—everything is very hush-hush, of course) about the liberal leanings of the bishop of Richmond, Virginia, who was thereupon treated to an inquisitive visit from the archbishop of St. Louis, representing the Vatican. That summer the archbishop of Zambia, whose faith healing had been tattled to Rome, received a visit from a Vatican cardinal and was soon on his way to the Vatican for rehabilitation and reassignment. Earlier, El Salvador's Archbishop Oscar Romero, who had had the audacity to protest against the rapacity of the right-wing establishment, was similarly visited shortly before his assassination by right-wing agents in 1980.

And then there's the case of Seattle's Archbishop Raymond Hunthausen. In 1981, about six years after his appointment to the Seattle archdiocese, he attracted some national attention with a speech delivered to a Lutheran synod deploring Seattle's role in harboring nuclear weapons. Because of the local Trident submarine base, he compared the situation to the Nazi death camps, warning that the people of the city and the state "must take special responsibility for what is in our backyard." Later he refused to pay a part of his income taxes in protest against government spending on arms. (He did pay up eventually, at the formidable insistence of the Internal Revenue Service.)

Such words and actions must have gravely offended Seattle Catholics suffering from Red Menace paranoia. Vatican mail bags must have must have bulged with indignant reports not only about Hunthausen's prostration before the evil empire but also about his permissiveness in running the diocese. He allowed

a group of homosexuals to attend Mass in the cathedral because
he holds to the current hierarchical consensus that, while homosexual acts are sinful, the homosexual condition is not, and he
was by no means obliged to assume the worst about those attending the Mass or to subject them to an ad hoc inquisition on
their individual behavior. This charitable decision apparently
induced a foam-flecked fury in others more judgmental. Although
never advocating abortion, he managed to infuriate right-to-life
ideologues by his failure to show proper enthusism for their tactics.

And then there were the liturgical shenanigans introduced
by some of his farther-out priests and parishioners. At one funeral
the parents of the deceased, a young man who had left behind
a wife and two children, were shocked to see some of the participants in the ceremony enter the nave of the church with joyful
shouts. The people attending were then asked to introduce themselves, rotary style. After the Mass, in which both Catholics and
non-Catholics received communion, a dancer floated by in front
of the congregation and a clown pranced happily about the coffin, festooning it with balloons. To conclude the festivities the
coffin was borne to the deceased's pickup truck by pallbearers
in workclothes. Since the widow had played the clown, this
presumably was the kind of ceremony wanted by the lately departed's closest relatives. But it left the widow's mother in tears,
and it must have generated a hot report to the Roman sentinels.
Hunthausen received a letter from Rome outlawing liturgical
dancing (and doubtless liturgical clowning), and he had the honor
of being branded a "false bishop" by *The Wanderer,* an irritably
archconservative Catholic weekly published in St. Paul.

In the fall of 1983 he also received an apostolic visit from

Archbishop James Hickey of Washington, D.C., a reputedly liberal prelate also opposed to the nuclear arms race. Rome had ordered the visit "so that it might evaluate the criticism and support the archbishop in his ministry." Hickey would make the visit "as a brother bishop to observe the situation at first hand and to offer fraternal assistance and support." The interference was awash with benevolence and brotherly love. While Hickey was interviewing various members of the archdiocese, a petition supporting Hunthausen was signed by 252 of his 280 priests. Finally the report was signed, sealed and delivered to Rome. Especially *sealed.* Hickey would not reveal its contents, but he did say "it wasn't easy."

As usual, it would be quite a while before any reaction would surface. Meanwhile another reaction did surface, arising from an incident of seven years earlier. The incident was Hunthausen's granting an imprimatur, a bishop's permission to publish, to a book entitled *Sexual Morality,* written by a professor of moral theology and published in 1977 by the Paulist Press. The publisher considered the book moderate in viewpoint and had never received a complaint against any of its 28,000 copies. The Roman doctrinaires disagreed, however, and in the spring of 1984 ordered Hunthausen to withdraw his imprimatur, admonishing him that "the imprimatur is to be granted only to those works which completely agree with official church teaching." (For "church" read "Roman"—and note where the word "completely" lays the burden of proof for anyone but a parrot.) He obeyed, asking that the imprimatur be omitted from future editions.

He was similarly orthodox in his response, also in 1984, to complaints that a Catholic hospital under his jurisdiction was performing sterilizations for purposes of contraception. He asked that it stop, and it stopped.

A reaction to the Hickey report, and doubtless other reports, arrived in Seattle in December 1985 in a letter from Archbishop Pio Laghi, Rome's apostolic delegate to the United States. "You and your collaborators," it conceded, "have suffered from exaggerated and mean-spirited criticism." To help him respond, it offered "certain guidance and advice" in a spirit of benevolent reformation. Hunthausen made the letter public, together with a letter of his own to be read in the churches reminding parishioners of Christ's repeated reassurance, "Do not be afraid." The "Lord is with us on each step of the journey," he concluded. "Knowing that and knowing too of your deep faith and loving support, I take courage for the future and look forward to the journey we will continue together."

This might have ended the affair if someone had not discovered a new use for a clause in the recently revised code of canon law, a clause allowing for the appointment of an auxiliary bishop with special powers. It had been used earlier to help bishops in financial difficulties, but it also could be used to humiliate a bishop by ordering him to turn over some of his authority to his auxiliary. And so it was that in the late summer of 1986 Hunthausen was instructed to cede his decision-making authority to his auxiliary bishop, Donald Wuerl, in the areas of treatment of ex-priests, training of priests, marriage regulation, and moral supervision of homosexuals and of health-care establishments. Because it was unprecedented, the order was especially offensive to most Seattle Catholics, who agreed with their archbishop that "as a diocese, we are not terribly different from many others."

Indeed, a Jesuit priest engaged in a study of American archdioceses, Thomas Reese, concurred and went a step further, reporting that "no evidence has been presented to show that Seattle is substantially different from other dioceses in the United States."

Presenting evidence is not very high on Rome's list of responsibilities. Neither Hunthausen nor Wuerl were given any reason for the order. Both men were confused but seem to have emerged from their initial shock in a spirit of cooperation. The last thing the archdiocese needed, Hunthausen cautioned publicly, was to be split into factions; everyone should try to make the new arrangement as effective as possible. There was reason to think that this could be done, since no one could discern any conspicuous aberrations remaining in the areas specified. There might be no reason to expect any further harassment of Hunthausen, unless it was simply that Somebody Up There had it in for him.

Letters to Hunthausen ran 99% in his favor. A petition from more than 13,000 Seattle Catholics protested the "injustice" and urged Rome to restore his full authority. The Canon Law Society of America, during its meeting that autumn, voted 173 to 53 to question whether Hunthausen's mistreatment conformed with canon law and to express its concern to the national bishops' conference and to Rome through the apostolic delegate. But the real question was whether any of this could have any effect on Somebody Up There, and perhaps it did. In May 1987, after a four-month study by a three-bishop commission, Rome announced that Hunthausen would be given back his full authority as bishop *but* would have a new coadjutor (assistant) bishop appointed by Rome, whom it would be "prudential" for him to consult on precarious matters. Hunthausen was "perceived as generating, or at least accepting, a climate of *permissiveness*" (italics added) and had demonstrated a lack of "the firmness necessary to govern the archdiocese." Incidentally, John Paul was scheduled to come to the West Coast during a big PR visit to the States in September, and no disharmony should mar the general ecstasy.

*   *   *

Raymond G. Hunthausen was born in August 1921 in Anaconda, Montana, educated at Carroll College in Helena, and trained at St. Edward's Seminary in Kenmore, Washington. He later attended St. Louis, Catholic, Fordham and Notre Dame Universities. Ordained priest in June 1946, he was consecrated bishop of Helena in August 1962 and was made archbishop of Seattle in February 1975. Inadvertently, it would seem.

Joseph Ratzinger

In the general confrontation between John Paul & Co. and the mavericks, the "& Co." has consisted most conspicuously of the cardinal in charge of the Congregation for the Doctrine of the Faith, Joseph Ratzinger, who is profiled here. The profile might have been offered earlier, immediately after that of John Paul, but it seemed more suitable, at least symbolically, to have the mavericks situated between the two prelates, as in the jaws of a vise.

The story of Joseph Ratzinger resembles that of Giovanni Mastai-Ferretti, who as the controversial Pope Pius IX reigned from 1846 to 1878 and produced the formal doctrine of papal infallibility as well as the notorious *Syllabus of Errors*. Both men, at least, underwent a similar transformation, not unlike Luther's reaction to the Peasants' Revolt. Pius started off his unseemly incumbency with a number of liberal reforms like press freedoms and lay councils, but the violent liberal revolutions of 1848, especially in Italy, turned him into an irascible reactionary.

Ratzinger before Vatican II was reputedly a liberal, but the violent student rebellions of the late 1960s, when he was theology dean at the University of Tübingen, taught him "where discussion must stop, because it is turning into a lie, and resistance must begin in order to maintain freedom." Or so he told E. J. Dionne Jr. of the New York *Times* in the fall of 1985. (For "resistance" read "repression.")

People have marveled at the change in his viewpoint. Hans Küng has commented that his later "self-righteous blindness" is "something one would not have thought possible in the light of the remarkable theological work which this man produced in the sixties." The surprise may have arisen partly out of reading his earlier work through rose-colored glasses. In 1962 he wrote in support of collegiality—but only as subject to papal supremacy. In *The Open Circle* (1966) he asked, "Does not our actual Christian reality resemble more the Jewish hierarchism castigated by Jesus than the picture he gave of Christian brotherhood?" The question sounds rhetorical, but he hastened to underline its irreverence: "The New Testament clearly differentiates the authorized representative who continues the mission of Jesus in an official capacity from the ordinary believers who are not so authorized. What we call 'the hierarchy' and 'the priesthood' are New Testament realities." Like John Paul, he early on understood The Truth and felt the urge to enlighten others. He was not, he told Dionne, "able to keep for myself the knowledge which seemed so important to me. The beautiful thing in it was the possiblity of giving it to others." Solicited or, perhaps, otherwise. For preachers, happiness is a captive audience.

In the same book, subtitled "The Meaning of Christian

Brotherhood," he generously shared his insight that the Christian, though loving all who are in need, "is the brother of his fellow Christian, but not of the non-Christian." In accord with his hero St. Paul, he demanded that "Christians must strive for the greatest possible independence from non-Christians and not choose them for their habitual companions. In fact, they should have as little as possible to do with them." Except for giving The Truth to others: a Christian's first duty "is that of missionizing."

In his book on Vatican II (also 1966) he seemed to view religious liberty with a kind of gingerly ambivalence. "Freedom is a vulnerable thing, which can easily destroy itself if used without restriction," he wrote, adding that "there are no sure norms or standards here." Evidently he found some later. The notion of "the Church of the poor" he considered "essentially sound," although he warned against a "sentimentality [that] could lead to a kind of romanticizing of poverty." Yet when it came to sentimentality, he was no slouch. "In the final analysis the Church lives, in sad as well as joyous times, from the faith of those who are simple of heart." Whatever the meaning of "simple of heart," his later attitudes suggest that he may initially have written "simple of head."

In his own case the heart seems to have been given preference over the head: the Church attracted him, for instance, through "the beauty of its liturgy." Early in his scholarly, mystical *Introduction to Christianity* he defined belief as "the trustful placing of myself on a ground that bears me up," which "cannot possibly be anything but the truth revealing itself." This follows revelations that belief is undemonstrable, a "risky enterprise of accepting what plainly cannot be seen as the truly real and fundamental."

Indeed, "the believer is choked by the salt water of doubt constantly washed into his mouth by the ocean of uncertainty." But evidently the ocean can be crossed by the leap of faith, leaving all uncertainty behind.

Ratzinger had left it far behind, at least professionally, by August 1984, some thirty months after his appointment to the doctrinal Congregation. In a long interview with Italian journalist Vittorio Messori, a breathless admirer who the next year published the interview as *The Ratzinger Report,* he explained the immutability of The Truth. Everyone was quite mistaken in thinking that his views had changed: "It is not I who have changed, but others"—others who departed from Vatican II "around 1973" to pave the way for a Vatican III, leaving his truth-promoting, homogeneous Church of today for a visionary, heterogeneous Church of tomorrow. Severing his connection with the "progressive" theological journal *Concilium,* he found refuge in "the conviction of the Church that there is *one truth,* and that this one truth can as such be recognized, expressed, and also clearly defined within certain bounds." (For "certain" read "indefinite.") A profound believer in an activist Satan, he also detected sinister impulses in assertions by more independent thinkers: "I wonder at the adroitness of theologians who manage to represent the exact opposite of what is written in the clear documents of the Magisterium in order afterward to set forth this inversion with skilled dialectical devices as the 'true' meaning of the document in question."

Partly as a result of such adroitness, the results of Vatican II deeply disappointed him. The "progressive process of decadence" following the council had largely discredited it. The decadence could be seen in the decline of theological forelock-pulling, in a lack of reverence for the basic structures of the Church, which "are willed by God himself, and therefore they are inviolable." Rome's authority comes from that of Christ, and this simple fact must be accepted as a prerequisite to the rediscovery of "the necessity and fruitfulness of obedience to the legitimate ecclesiastical authorities." Authorities, that is, in proper subjection to Rome; conferences of bishops, for instance, although they "have . . . a practical, concrete function," are peripheral, "do not belong to the structure of the Church as willed by Christ."

Episcopal conferences, indeed, are worrisome, since they tend to emit opinions without proper supervision. It is better for bishops not to band together, better for them to be individually accountable (to we all know whom). No closing of ranks. This avoids opinions being watered down to accommodate majorities, special interests, lowest common denominators. In prewar Germany, Ratzinger asserted, the conference of bishops proved weak in opposing Nazism, while the strong criticism "came from individual courageous bishops." He avoided any further analogies.

Such bishops are needed today, but in the wake of Vatican II, during the heyday of its liberal interpretations, the episcopacy was diluted by the appointment of bishops who were "open to the world" but who were unable to oppose it and its undesirable tendencies or to "warn the faithful against them." Such bishops have been abetted by "creative" theologians, although a theologian's duty to the deposit of faith preserved in Rome is to deepen understanding of it, to help proclaim it, "not 'to create' it."

For Ratzinger, the world is the Church's adversary, not its friend. It has, for instance, separated sex from procreation, and this has led to the gratification of base instincts "no longer subject to rational restraints." It is a world in which *Humanae Vitae*, Paul VI's birth-control encyclical, "has not been understood." It is thus a world in which sexuality has become "the sole point of reference in the will of the person." It is a world influenced by Marxism, so that in many liberation theologies the absolute good has become "the building of a just socialist society," justifying when necessary "violence, homicide, mendacity." Thus a theoretical liberation, described glowingly in words, "shows its diabolical visage in deeds." It is a world in which religious vocations have dropped steeply, especially among women: in very Catholic Quebec, a decline in new vocations between 1961 and 1981 of almost 99%! This is appalling, but there is some comfort in the fact that among cloistered nuns, relatively shut away from flesh and devil, the situation is less unnerving. It is a world in which straw men are black or white, rarely grey.

It is a world which prates of liberation from economic slavery but denies "the radical slavery of sin," ignoring The Truth or watering it down. Why, for example, has the idea of purgatory been relegated to the back burner? "The fact is that all of us today think we are so good that we deserve nothing less than heaven!" (The word "fact," the phrase "all of us," and the exclamation point all appear in the text.) Does the idea of purgatory come from the Bible? What difference does *that* make? It is a part of Catholic tradition. And since "the Gospels are a product of the early Church," it is perfectly obvious that "the whole of Scripture is nothing other than tradition."

It is not unreasonable to think of Ratzinger's mind as one of the sharpest minds of the 13th century, which a Jesuit historian has called "the greatest of centuries." He surely seems better suited to a time when a dominant hierarchy could see to it that the simple-minded faithful totally believed and dutifully did what they were told. On the other hand, he is not unaware or utterly contemptuous of history. In his *Introduction to Christianity* he approvingly quoted the description of the Church by William of Auvergne, bishop of Paris in that century: "William said that the barbarism of the Church must make everyone who saw it grow rigid with horror: 'Bride she is no more, but a monster of frightful ugliness and ferocity. . . .'"

For the 20th century, however, Ratzinger remains the rigid authoritarian, ostensibly quite confident in the inerrancy of his pronouncements, the justice of his treatment of others, and the duty of his divinely appointed inferiors to obey. It may be significant to note how he quotes St. Paul's advice to proselytizers. Most translations of 2 Timothy 4:2 use words like *reprove, rebuke, exhort;* or *convince, reproach, encourage;* or *correct, reprove, appeal.* Ratzinger's preference, as given in the Messori interview, is, "Refute falsehood, correct error, call to obedience."

*   *   *

Joseph Ratzinger was born April 1927 in Marktyl am Inn, Bavaria. As a youth he was protected from the allurements of Nazism by his sturdy faith in Roman Catholicism, whose liturgy he found esthetically irresistible and whose "secret of truth" he found intellectually attractive.

After graduation from the University of Munich, answering a call from God, who "wanted something from me," he was ordained a priest in 1951. For about the next quarter century he taught theology successively, and very successfully, at the universities of Freising, Bonn, Münster, Tübingen, and Regensburg. In addition, he became a prolific author of books on various aspects of Catholic faith and morals. Their scholarship and mystical perceptions earned him a reputation, which in turn earned him an appointment, at Vatican II between 1962 and 1965, as theological consultant to Cardinal Joseph Frings. This far-sighted cardinal, among other things, cooperated with some other bishops in a group effort to stymie the Roman doctrinaires' anti-reform program. Ratzinger himself cooperated with such liberals as Hans Küng and Karl Rahner, joining in a condemnation of the Holy Office, predecessor of his present Congregation, and describing it as "detrimental to the faith."

Three years later, in 1968, the leftist rebellions on European and U.S. campuses turned his attitude toward Marxism from a wary curiosity into implacable hostility. Marxism, he concluded with the fervor of a convert, for all its emphasis on workers losing their chains, was really a hypocritical and radical "attack on human freedom and dignity." His hostility percolated into a concern over leftist leanings in the Church, which he felt were transforming the vigorous renewal of Vatican II into an ineffectual yet perilous decadence.

In 1977, having been made archbishop of Munich and Freising by Paul VI, he attended an episcopal synod where he met a man of like mind, Cardinal Karol Wojtyla of Cracow, whose experience with Marxism in Poland had convinced him that any talk of freedom arising out of class struggle could lead only to "an illusory earthly liberation." Both men felt that the

Church badly needed a return to The Truth and a restoration of authority and discipline. The following year Wojtyla became Pope John Paul II.

Meanwhile Ratzinger had made cardinal, and in November 1981 John Paul appointed him to head the Congregation for the Doctrine of the Faith, on which the new pope depended for a vigorous imposition of Roman orthodoxy. The rest is recent history.

For its burdensome task the Congregation consists of only thirty people, not nearly enough. This staff shortage is not universally lamented.

A Papal Tradition

The Vatican is chock-full of "holy" offices and "sacred" congregations; the odor of self-appointed sanctity can be downright overpowering. Living in that odor morning, noon and night is a fairly small cluster of men entitled to address one another as "Your Eminence" and "Your Grace"—and, in one particular case, "Your Holiness," this being reserved for "the Holy Father." In such an environment they can be expected to have a group self-image of seraphim proportions.

There are many kinds of holiness, and the Vatican has had its share. As for the reputation of Their Holinesses, Catholic apologists have made much of the distinction between the office and the man; excepting the first fifty, relatively few popes have been officially declared to have been saints. But amid the traditional bowing and scraping, the hands clasped in prayer and raised in benediction, the distinction grows very soft and fuzzy. If papal reverence for Our Predecessors of Happy Memory is made the basis for requiring catatonic obedience, and it is, it may also excite some curiosity, at least among the historically oriented, about just how Happy that Memory really is.

The answer is, not very. Their Holinesses generally can be credited with a less unsavory record than Their Majesties, but then few Majesties have laid any special claim to Holiness. At times, notably in the tenth and sixteenth centuries, the shenanigans in the Holy See have made American scandals like Teapot Dome, Watergate and Iranscam seem like the frolicking of cherubs in Paradise Park. And so a stroll down memory lane may be appropriate here to remind us that papal tradition includes some Holy Fathers whose conduct has raised eyebrows and, on occasion, hair.

JOHN XII (955-63)

Around 750 A.D. a papal official wrote a fanciful last will and testament attributed to the Roman Emperor Constantine and deeding "our palaces, the City of Rome, and all the provinces, places and cities of Italy and the regions of the West to the most blessed pontiff and Universal Pope"—although the title of pope was not accorded the bishop of Rome until two centuries after Constantine's death. Despite this chronological discrepancy, the "Donation of Constantine" was generally accepted as authentic, making the papacy a coveted prize among the noble hoodlum families scheming and fighting for political control in the capital of western Christianity. And to make the document effective as well as generally accepted, the Frankish kings Pepin and Charlemagne established its terms quite persuasively by force of arms.

They also introduced some law and order in Rome for a while, but as Frankish power waned in Italy the Roman hoodlums resumed their incessant hostilities. In March 896, for instance, the leader of one faction, having managed to get himself installed as Pope Stephen VII, had the body of a predecessor named Formosus, spawn of a rival faction, exhumed and put on public trial before a holy synod (yes, physically). His Late Holiness was found guilty of uncanonical conduct after a raging prosecution by His Present Holiness. The ex-holy corpse was thereupon disrobed, after its blessing fingers had been amputated, and turned over to a mob for unceremonious disposal in the Tiber. Some days later it was buried under more edifying circumstances by some sympathetic nonclerical fishermen.

Although elsewhere in the world some decency was being introduced by the reforms of Cluny, these obviously were brutish times in Rome, and many popes simply failed to rise above them, in some cases barely to their level. An illustration of the casual brutality is the murder of three successive popes between 928 and 931, and an illustration of papal accommodation is the eight-year reign of His Holiness Pope John XII.

In the early 900s a papal official named Theophylact set up a family dynasty that dominated Roman politics, civil and papal, for half a century before subsiding into rival-gang status. Around 937 (chronicles of this period are known for neither meticulous accuracy nor strict impartiality) his son Alberic produced a son, Octavian, who at the age of sixteen succeeded his father as Prince of Rome. Alberic had extracted a solemn promise from the noble Roman senators to elect his son pope. About a year after his death the reigning pope died accommodatingly, and Octavian became John XII (pagan names for popes were going out of style).

His New Young Holiness evidently was a rather charming rascal who would prove himself to be a fairly adroit con man in his dealings with rival hoodlums. Devoted to hunting, he heightened the pleasure of his devotions by ordaining several of his fellow huntsmen to the priesthood, presumably to make them more eligible for room and board in the Lateran palace (forerunner of the Vatican palace). To enhance the pleasure of their company, he added the delights of gambling and assorted female ministrations.

Although barely literate and noted for his primitive grammar, John XII had a talent for political scheming. His scheme for protecting his Constantinian estates from Berengar, the acquisitive king of Italy (then a realm in the north), was to call on the Saxon king Otto for help. Otto, perhaps the most powerful chieftain in Europe and repeller of Huns, was happy to oblige. He arrived exuberantly in Italy in 961 at the head of an army larger and more ruffian than Berengar's. His Holiness welcomed him by crowning him Holy Roman Emperor, a sacrilegious title that would bend many a reverential knee over the next nine centuries. But within a couple of weeks the welcome had worn uncomfortably thin.

The trouble was that Otto suffered from at least a mild case of Teutonic austerity. Before leaving on an expedition to crush Berengar and restore whatever papal lands the Italian had appropriated, Otto spent two weeks, off and on, lecturing His Holiness on the need to mend his profligate ways. This so exasperated the profligate that, immediately after Otto's departure, His Holiness began scheming against him. He sent a message to Berengar, of all people, offering to make *him* emperor if he would rid Italy of the Dutch uncle. The offer was as futile as it was treacherous, for Berengar had all he could do to maintain some dignity while retreating. Before the Holy Father was finished, he had made similarly futile offers to Berengar's son, to the Huns, and to the Byzantines. No one wanted to take on the mighty Saxon.

Eventually the Saxon, getting wind of all this feverish activity, sent an envoy to Rome to find out what His Holiness was up to, and the envoy returned with a papal complaint that Otto was taking his sweet time returning the rest of the papal estates. Otto could accept this affront with equanimity, but he had learned that Berengar's son had decided to take the papal offer after all and was already in Rome, his head itching for the crown. This gave Otto the incentive he needed to march on Rome. At the news of his approach the Holy Father buckled on his best defensive armor and hastily retired to Tivoli, some fifteen miles east of Rome.

Three days later Otto, in command of Rome and evidently having concluded that His Holiness was a tad unreliable, convoked a council. After hearing a litany of colorful accusations, the assembled bishops sent a summons to His Holiness to come and defend himself. He replied in a letter admirable for its directness and brevity if not for its grammar: "To all the bishops: We hear you wish to make another pope. If you do I excommunicate you by almighty God and you have no power to ordain no one or celebrate Mass." The bishops' reply was similarly direct: come to Rome or *you'll* be excommunicated.

Otto had had it with His Holiness, who was deposed in December 963 and replaced with a Leo VIII. But once again the Saxon warlord had to leave Rome to deal with the Berengar gang. So the irrepressible John returned, deposing and excommunicating his replacement in a hastily called rump council. (Leo had already taken a precipitous powder.) He then set about restoring Church discipline. A hand was chopped off here, a tongue was torn out there, noses and fingers were amputated, backs were zealously scourged.

Otto, busy with Berengar (and now saddled with Leo), at first could do nothing about the situation. Meanwhile the Romans elected a new Holiness, Benedict V, in May 964. The next month Otto returned and reinstated Leo. By now John XII was dead. The stories of his demise, although varying in detail, seem to converge into a simple account: on his way to visit his mistress the Holy Father was murdered by her husband.

BENEDICT IX (1032-46)

As the 900s passed boisterously into the year 1000—without a second coming of Christ, to the surprise and perhaps the relief of Christian numerologists—the house of Theophylact remained a power in Rome, although the power was often exercised from its baronial headquarters in Tusculum, about fifteen miles to the southeast. By this time the Theophylacts' presiding don was Count Gregory, grandson or great-grandson of the founding Theophylact. His title had been conferred by Otto's grandson, Otto III, Holy Roman Emperor No. 3. In return the count, whose faithfulness as an ally matched that of John XII, drove the young Otto out of Rome. For good measure he also drove out the German-born Sylvester II; that good pope's basic honesty and learned intelligence must have been infuriating.

Sylvester's death in 1003 was followed by a decade of revolving-door papacies. In 1012 a Count Theophylactus was forcibly elected Benedict VIII; although his foremost interest was in sword and scepter, he did introduce some church reforms under pressure from Emperor Henry II. After his death (unspectacular) in 1024, he was succeeded by his hastily ordained younger brother Count Romanus, whose first interest as John XIX was more along the lines of accumulating wealth, since his purchase of the Holy See had drained much of his resources. Although he supported some reforms outside Rome, he leaned within it toward a vigorous practice of simony; on one occasion his Holiness was deterred only by public outcry from selling the papal primacy to the Patriarch of Byzantium.

His death around the end of 1032 brought on another liberally financed papal election. In this one his nephew, fifteen-year-old Count Theophylactus, became Benedict IX. Six months later His Pubescent Holiness was forced out of Rome by threats of assassination, but he soon showed a notable ability to bounce back. After his return he enjoyed three years of emergent woman-izing which incited the Romans into a violent revolt, and again His Holiness fled the city, this time to the protection of Conrad, an up-and-coming German chieftain. Conrad was headed toward Rome, although at the moment he was busy dealing with the intervening Lombards in northern Italy. After overcoming their inhospitality (and that of the archbishop of Milan, whom his Holiness compliantly excommunicated), he entered Rome and reinstalled his new papal buddy.

This time the papal frolics lasted two years, at the end of which Conrad & Co. had to go about their business elsewhere, leaving the Romans to express their pique in another uprising.

His Holiness retired hurriedly to the protection of his uncle, don of Tusculum. In his absence a local bishop bought the papal crown from the electors and was declared Sylvester III. His Latest Holiness perched nervously on the papal throne for only three precarious months, however, for Benedict had returned by then with avuncular force. Sylvester took to the Sabine Hills.

But then Benedict began having some sober second thoughts about the papacy as a way of life. Indeed, he was becoming concerned about its being a way of death, by violence, and he decided to give it up. There may have been another reason, which was the talk of Rome at the time: His Holiness had fallen in love and wanted to get married, but the girl's father had insisted that he resign first, on the grounds that no respectable father could let his daughter marry anything so disreputable as a pope.

Resigning meant giving up the comforts of the papal income, so His Holiness cast about for a way to make some money first. He found one: he sold the papacy for 1500 pounds of gold to Giovanni Gratiano, a local priest and his godfather, a good man who stooped to simony to rid his beloved Church of this carbuncle, and who thereupon became Gregory VI. Benedict, promising to leave him alone, took to the Alban Hills. But he and his immediate predecessors had rendered the papacy so poor and powerless, and Rome so chaotic and turbulent, that Gregory had no real opportunity to improve things—especially since Benedict and Sylvester *both* showed up in Rome within two years, trying simultaneously to plant their papal bottoms on the papal throne.

This time the Romans, instead of carrying rebellion into the streets, carried an appeal to the emperor, who came to Rome and called an ecclesiastical council. The exasperated council formally deposed all three Holinesses, including even Gregory, for whom they had considerable respect. But as soon as the emperor left Rome, Benedict was back again, perhaps disappointed in marriage if not in love. The newly elected Clement was shouldered aside. Eight months later, early in 1045, back came the Germans, and this time His Holiness left town for good. A council deposed him, or disposed of him, in 1046. The most charitable account of his end has him entering a monastery in a fit of repentance and there spending the rest of his life nursing his holiness.

BONIFACE VIII (1294-1303)

Over the next 150 years the papacy continued its traditionally checkered career, consisting neither of unrelieved venality and corruption nor of uninterrupted effectiveness and holiness. Popes came and went, sometimes with staggering rapidity, with gaps between them often of months and occasionally of years. They included able reformers like Gregory VII and saintly incompetents like Celestine V, and generally were a motley crew caught in the incessant struggle among Roman, German, French and other predators for control of papal pomp, panoply, prestige, power and property.

It was Celestine V who treated Rome to one of the papacy's more bizarre episodes. It was 1294, and by this time popes had come to be elected by a college of Roman cardinals. The previous pope had died in April 1292, but the cardinals, evenly split in their loyalties to the Orsini and Colonna clans, were still debating the election of a successor in the summer of 1294 when they received a message from a hermit named Peter of Morone flaying them for the delay. He was in his mid-eighties and couldn't last very long, so the exhausted cardinals elected *him*. He was utterly appalled but was persuaded by disciples to take the job and try to invest it with some Christian virtues. He took the job in July, made a mess of it, and resigned in December. This opened the way for a cardinal named Benedict Gaetani, who had been busily ingratiating himself with both rival clans, to get himself elected as Boniface VIII.

After a coronation ceremony laden with richly ostentatious symbolism, His Holiness spent much of 1295 directing the pursuit of the ex-papal hermit, who was hiding out in mountain fastnesses and who even tried to escape from Italy. Both men knew that the hermit's partisans were declaring his resignation invalid. The hermit was fleeing to prevent any possibility of his returning to the papal throne, and the pope was after him for the same reason. In August 1295 pope captured hermit and stowed him safely away in a small cell of a castle until the harassed victim died the following May. Seventeen years later the hermit was canonized St. Celestine V.

His Holiness Boniface VIII was a real family man, not a spawner of children like some others flaunting the mantle of St. Peter, but a man dedicated to the generous accumulating of family wealth. The Gaetani clan was one of modest means, and something would have to be done about *that*. Something was. A fourth of the papal revenue was devoted to greatly augmenting Gaetani properties in cities and rural areas stretching well to the south of Rome, to the consternation of rival clans, especially the Colonnas. The consternation and rivalry peaked in May 1297 when Stephen Colonna helped himself to a caravan of gold-laden mules headed for papal headquarters. Although the two older and less impulsive Colonnas in the college of cardinals persuaded their young kinsman to return the loot, His Holiness demanded that papal troops be quartered in all the Colonnas' principal towns, giving the two cardinals five days to reply.

The reply came four days later, after a hurried family conference, in the form of posters nailed to the doors of churches in Rome (plus one impudently left on the main altar of St. Peter's). The papal election had been fraudulent, the posters argued (his predecessor then being still alive), and a general council should be called to clear things up. His Holiness responded with a grandiloquent papal bull ("In Excelso Throno") in which he fired and excommunicated the two cardinals. *They* replied with a complementary accusation of murdering his Predecessor of Happy Memory. *He* responded with another bull excommunicating the cardinals' entire family to the fourth generation, making them vulnerable to any attack by anyone without penalty. Desperately they appealed to France and to anyone else who would listen to their emissaries, but to no avail.

Emboldened by their failure, His Holiness in September encouraged raids on Colonna properties by absolving from sin all thieves who had looted the clan's houses in Rome. Toward the end of 1297 he called for a holy crusade, permitting him to collect money everywhere in Christendom, especially in exchange for indulgences. Since the crusade was universally recognized as merely a local vendetta, the response to this spiritual extortion was meager, except from a few Colonnaphobes like the Orsinis. Yet his call was effective in releasing "crusaders" from any discrimination in attacking not only the Colonna family members but also others— servants, peasants, tradesmen—connected with them.

By the fall of 1298 the crusade had taken all the Colonnas' cities but one, their home base of Palestrina. It was considered practically impregnable, but a little guile can do wonders. His Holiness sent a message to the Colonnas clustered within its walls that he would pardon them and let bygones be bygones if they would just surrender. Naively, they did—and he did, except that their cities remained in the possession of his allies and that he utterly destroyed Palestrina, one of Christendom's most splendid cities. The Colonnas dispersed to bide their time while nursing their revenge.

Much of the following year was devoted to preparing Christendom's first grand jubilee welcoming the turn of a century. Indulgences were granted for coming to Rome to visit Holy Places, thereby enriching papal coffers with tourist ducats. Although Europe's monarchs and nobility proved uninterested, uncounted thousands of pilgrims crowded into Rome to spend their money on such worthy causes as might be brought to their pious attention. They were not affluent enough, however, to make the jubilee as golden as had been hoped.

The next year, 1301, Boniface tangled with Philip the Fair of France, who had decided to tax the wealth of French monasteries to help finance his incessant warring against England and European barons. His Holiness reacted with a bull forbidding the taxing of any clergy without his permission, but Philip retaliated with a decree prohibiting the export of money, including Church income going to Rome, and expelling foreign residents such as papal representatives. Boniface had met his match; he backed down, and the two willful men settled into an uneasy compromise until the end of the year. The controversy then flared up again, with His Holiness making the usual spiritual threats and His Majesty mockingly addressing him as "Your Fatuity." In 1302 His Majesty called together a national council to defame His Holiness, who retaliated by calling together a Church council to assert absolute papal supremacy, spiritual and temporal. To emphasize his point the pope included a solemn declaration: "We declare, state, define and pronounce that it is altogether necessary for salvation for every human creature to be subject to the Roman pontiff." This dogmatic assertion would ring infallibly through succeeding centuries until the twentieth, when it would be flatly contradicted by two popes and a Vatican Council.

The summer of 1303 found His Holiness in his home town of Anagni, some thirty-seven miles from the miasmal heat of violence-ridden Rome. One day early in September a French-financed gang of well-armed ruffians entered the town, duping the town militia into thinking that they were a delegation to summon the pope to a council. They then entered the papal palace, easily dispersed the pope's nephews who were standing guard, and found a forewarned Boniface sitting grandly and bravely on the papal throne, decked out to meet his end in all his finery. The gang leader, a choleric Colonna survivor, would have stabbed him to death but for the intervention of a less emotional French co-conspirator. Instead, they held him prisoner until, after three days, the local militia and citizens woke up, set him free, and returned him to Rome. There he lasted only a month while enemy clans forcibly reclaimed his family's ill-gotten possessions.

The self-proclaimed spiritual and temporal ruler of the world died a self-imprisoned recluse in the Lateran palace. His successors roundly condemned the people of Anagni for failing to protect him.

URBAN VI (1378-89)

By 1376 seven popes had for 67 years held court in Avignon under the more or less benevolent protection of the French monarchy. But in that year, Pope Gregory XI, goaded by St. Catherine of Sienna, returned to Rome with his reluctant curia. In their company was one Bartolomeo Prignano, the curia's assistant chancellor and titular archbishop of Bari. In his late fifties, this stout little bureaucrat had every reason to feel that he had reached a dead end in a drab career. That career seems to have made him an unhappy man, since it kept him in the company of his official superiors, cardinals whose high living and low morals offended his dour rectitude, which in turn invited their jaundiced teasing.

Bartolomeo doubtless expected that Gregory, who died in 1378, would be succeeded by one of the French cardinals. Of the sixteen cardinal electors in Rome, after all, ten were French. But he had underestimated the persuasive powers of the riotous Roman mob, who expressed their preference for an Italian pope by breaking into a room beneath the cardinals' meeting room and threatening to build a bonfire unless their demand was met. Since none of the Italian cardinals could be elected, for labyrinthine political reasons, the electors desperately chose the unsuspecting bureaucrat in a hasty compromise. Though not a Roman, Bartolomeo was at least Italian, being originally from Naples, and Naples' Queen Joanna was partial to the French.

The sudden elevation seems to have affected his character. As Bartolomeo he had always been irascible; as Urban VI he became chronically, violently bad-tempered. At his first meeting with the cardinals His Holiness flew into and maintained such a high level of vituperative rage, venting his pent-up fury at their wealth and ostentation and corruption, that many witnesses thought he had gone at least temporarily mad. He sent Queen Joanna's envoys away angry by regaling them with gross insults about her character. Much, probably most of what he said in his fits of choler was probably accurate, but his way of saying it neither won friends nor influenced people. And he seemed to get worse each day.

By September, only five months after his election, the French cardinals elected a rival pope, Clement VII, a sterling character who as cardinal had ordered the massacre of 4000 residents of the little town of Cesena. Urban responded by creating a separate, very Italian College of Cardinals with associated curial bureaucracy, so that there were now two papal establishments, about evenly balanced in terms of political support. And thus the Church entered upon the forty years of its Great Schism, especially after Urban's mercenaries drove his rival out of Italy to Avignon.

His Roman Holiness now turned his attention to Naples, which he felt should be in friendlier hands to promote some nearby land-grabbing by a favored nephew. A baronial don, promised papal recognition, took the city and murdered its queen but then lost interest in securing land for the nephew. His Holiness, over his curial cardinals' protests, moved the papal court to Naples for supervisory purposes, but he was allowed to enter the city as a visitor and no more. Stymied, he moved on south to a suburb and set up court as though he intended to stay. The cardinals were so appalled that they began quietly discussing the feasibility of having this madman deposed or even burned as a heretic. Their heretic-elect, however, getting wind of the plot, ordered the six chief conspirators arrested, tortured for several days, and executed. The only one of the six to survive was the English cardinal, courtesy of irresistible pressure from his king, Richard II. This incident has been considered as an especially heinous one because the six victims were *cardinals*.

Urban eventually did get back to Rome, where he spent his last year, dying in 1389. Twenty years later the Roman and Avignon cardinals proved desperate enough to unite in a single council, in which they declared both popes deposed and elected a new one. But popes can be stubborn, so that now, instead of two Holinesses, there were three.

ALEXANDER VI (1492-1503)

By 1492 the Church had been unified under a single papacy for 75 years. Its income now converged on the Renaissance papal establishment, growing heavy with an opulence of art treasures. Within less than half a century not merely Catholicism or Christendom but Christianity itself would be fragmented into warring factions, yet the popes for the present were preoccupied with matters much dearer to their acquisitive hearts.

At first it seemed that a young Spaniard named Rodrigo Borgia might prove unsuited to Rome's atmosphere of competitive materialism. In 1455, when he was 24, an uncle of his had metamorphosed into Pope Calixtus III, bringing with him to Rome an unnerving horde of hungry Spanish relatives and acquaintances. Having adopted his two nephews Rodrigo and Pedro, he showered them with lucrative offices and titles, making Rodrigo a cardinal at 26 and then a vice-chancellor of the Church. While his uncle lived, the young man behaved himself so sensibly that a contemporary chronicler described him as seeming "older than his years." The death of Calixtus in 1460, however, changed things considerably. His successor, the Italian Pius II, could not or would not protect the honors-laden Pedro from the wrath of Roman adversaries, who managed to get him permanently exiled (he died soon thereafter). But Rodrigo was something else again: his vote as cardinal had tipped the balance for Pius, whose gratitude maintained him unscathed. Indeed, when His Eminence's conduct changed overnight, His Holiness merely remonstrated in a now famous letter, urging him among other things to stop arranging situations so "that your lusts might be given free rein." But later, on being informed that the reports were exaggerated, he apologized.

Rodrigo lost none of his profitable sinecures despite the pope's disapproval of his taste for orgasmic orgies, and so as he passed into his forties he was reputedly the second richest cardinal in Rome, a city crawling with rich cardinals. Yet he was not rich enough to buy the papacy outright when Pius died in 1484 and was succeeded by Innocent VIII. This Innocent was the first Holy Father to publicly recognize his bastard children: a daughter, and a son who profited hugely from his Holy Father's unbridled nepotism. By the time His Holiness entered into his reward in the summer of 1492, his example had paved the way for a loyal family man on the make.

By this time Rodrigo had accumulated the wherewithal needed to overcome his fellow cardinals' distaste for his Spanish blood and for his salivating eagerness in pursuit of the papal prize. He took the name Alexander VI in honor of the ancient Macedonian conqueror; Caesar was merely a mortal, some of his triumphant ceremonial banners proclaimed, but this Alexander is a God. After a lavishly costly inaugural celebration, His Holiness entered on a eleven-year reign characterized, in the words of a scholar from Florence, "by an insatiable greed, an overwhelming ambition and a burning passion for the advancement of his many children." Four of the children, including the notorious Cesare and the much defamed Lucrezia, were the progeny of his principal concubine, Vanozza de' Catani, whom he kept ostensibly respectable with three successive husbands, all generously remunerated. He was a large, stout, vigorous man now in his early sixties, inordinately attractive to women and evidently capable of satisfying them and himself till the end of his days.

His reign was eventful. One of its highlights was his futile appeal to a Moslem sultan for help against the French just before their abortive invasion of Italy. Another was an erotic ballet-like performance by naked courtesans attended by His Holiness with his favorite son and daughter. Another was his extreme reaction to his eldest son's murder, which he accepted as a scourge for his sins, promising his cardinals, "We are resolved to amend our life and reform the Church. We renounce all nepotism. We will start the reform with Ourself and so continue through all levels of the Church until the entire work is completed." Within six weeks a papal bull announcing severe reforms was drafted. It was never published and was soon forgotten.

Reform was hardly his overriding concern, as was illustrated in his treatment of Girolamo Savonarola. That celebrated Dominican friar, scourge of a corrupt Florence and of the Medicis, accused him of buying the papacy and then using it to enrich his family and live a life of luxury and license. His Holiness reacted in 1498 by having his unruly critic interrogated under unspeakable tortures and committed to the flames on charges consisting essentially of insubordination and heresy. The insubordination was obvious enough, but the charge of heresy was a canard.

Still another highlight of this Holy Father's reign was the triumphant conquest of Rome by son Cesare in 1500, another splendidly lucrative Jubilee Year. Cesare's insufferable tyranny promoted a relentless practice of simony and nepotism, facilitated by incarcerations and murders as needed (including the murder of Lucrezia's beloved young husband, who had become politically superfluous). While the princely son rode about Italy with an army, creating a Borgia empire, his Holy Father eagerly cooperated, providing funds and the subtler benefits of political maneuvering. The papal pair were riding high, yet within three years of the Holy Father's death in 1503, from malaria or perhaps from a poisoned meal, the son was fighting as a common mercenary in Spain, where he died in battle.

*   *   *

A word might be appropriately inserted here about Alexander's almost immediate successor, Julius II (1503-13). Although ordinarily not numbered among the "bad popes"—he was not personally corrupt, licentious, spectacularly greedy or intolerably philoprogenitive—he was typical of the age in being an Italian prince, politician, soldier, administrator and art patron who also happened to be pope. He joined France against Venice, and then Venice against France, personally leading his troops in his favorite attire, battle armor. He sponsored and supervised Raphael and Michelangelo, and he laid the foundation of the complex we know today as St. Peter's. Meanwile northern Europe was fast slipping away from the Church, irrevocably.

LEO X (1513-21)

Destined for a Church career virtually from birth, the boy was tonsured at the age of seven and made abbot of Font Douce at eight, of Pissigano at nine, and of Monte Carlo at eleven. At fourteen he was consecrated cardinal and at eighteen, after entering the Sacred College, he was appointed commander of the papal troops. Things like this came easily to him, for he was Giovanni, son of Lorenzo de Medici, Lorenzo the Magnificent, ruler of Florence.

As Leo X he began his reign by spending a seventh of the papal treasury in a single day on his coronation ceremony, in which he paraded on a magnificent white charger. Massively fat and short-legged, he rode well nonetheless, and perhaps his greatest pleasure as Holy Father was indulging his obsessive passion for hunting, despite the canonical ban against clerical hunting; the most favorable time to bring him a petition, it was said, was after a successful hunt. In autumn the papal party would regularly ride about Italy in pursuit of game birds, game fish, deer and wild boar. Between hunts His Holiness was the sterotypical Renaissance prince and lavish patron of the arts, including those of Raphael and Michelangelo and the creation of a new St. Peter's.

He was also stereotypically greedy for real estate. To give the duchy of Urbino to his nephew Lorenzo, he ordered the incumbent duke to turn it over forthwith and excommunicated him for noncompliance. The duke had befriended the Medicis, and Leo's brother had promised that Urbino would not be molested, but this was of no consequence to the Holy Father, who soon acquired the duchy with the help of French troops, installing the young Lorenzo as duke and captain-general. The necessary papers were countersigned in Rome by the entire Sacred College of Cardinals, the only exception being the bishop of Urbino, who left Rome with haste and circumspection. When the ousted duke, having gathered some troops for purposes of reinstatement, sent Lorenzo an envoy under safe-conduct to negotiate, the usurper seized the hapless emissary and dispatched him to Rome, where His Holiness had him tortured for the extraction of military intelligence. The duke, eventually deserted by his mercenaries, took to exile as the better part of valor.

That same year, 1517, His Holiness again used safe-conduct treachery and torture, this time to investigate a murder plot against him in the Sacred College. His reaction was practical rather than vindictive. Only the ringleading Eminence was tortured and hanged, with his unfortunate servants, while two others were fined and exiled. Soon thereafter Leo created 31 new cardinals in a move that not only was enormously profitable but also packed the college with red-capped supporters.

Throughout his reign Leo's biggest problem was money, which he needed to maintain and embellish the papal palace, to hold on to his mercenary troops, to collect and exhibit art treasures, to hunt and banquet extravagantly, to complete the magnificent

St. Peter's basilica. For all his vast financial resources, he was chronically in debt. And so he breathed new life into a practice common during the Crusades but lately rather neglected: the selling of indulgences, which allegedly spared the buyers at least some of the acute discomforts of a posthumous stopover in purgatory. The rest is familiar history: the tragedy of errors involving Johann Tetzel, the fanatic indulgence peddler whom His Holiness failed to control until it was too late, and Martin Luther, the enraged monk whom His Holiness could never understand.

CLEMENT VII (1523-34)

Leo's successor emerged out of compromise. A righteous Dutch theologian, he was a determined reformer deeply contemptuous of Roman depravity. He lasted only twenty months, to the worried cardinals' vast relief. After this fright the Sacred College would elect only Italian popes for the next 455 years.

He was succeeded by another scion of the Medici clan who would pay the price for centuries of papal corruption. His weakness was not womanizing, but temporizing. Caught between France's King Francis I and Spain's King (and Holy Roman Emperor) Charles V, Clement VII played shuttlecock in their badminton game in his desperate efforts to preserve the property of the Medici papacy. Neither Francis nor Charles was tempted to attack the other directly, but both lusted after Italian booty. In the fall of 1524 their two armies converged on Italy.

When Francis took Milan, the Holy Father recognized him as duke in return for a promise to keep his royal hands off the Papal States. This arrangement lasted only a few months.

In February 1525 Charles routed the French, imprisoned Francis, and asked for papal recognition. His Holiness, much relieved, eagerly complied, and spent the spring and summer plotting to suborn one of Charles's chief lieutenants, offering to crown him king of Naples if he would betray the emperor and join an alliance against him. But the lieutenant loyally revealed the plot, Clement's chief plotter was arrested, and Charles tightened his grip on Italy— yet, again to the Holy Father's puzzled relief, left the Papal States intact. Then in May 1526, after Charles had released Francis on his promise to renounce all claims to Italian territory, His Holiness approached Francis with an offer to release him from that promise if he would bring France into a holy alliance with Venice, Milan, and the Papal States.

Clement paid for his vacillation and treachery that September, when a cardinal from the Colonna clan led a large detachment of troops in an attack on Rome, exuberantly plundered it, and forced the now diffident pope to seek safety in the castle of Sant' Angelo. The next day, however, an ambassador from Charles appeared, and His Holiness eagerly signed another treaty, agreeing to pardon the Colonna interlopers and to desert the holy alliance, at least temporarily.

Less than four months later, in December, he was busily trying to patch up the holy alliance, but Charles had had enough of blessed betrayals, and by February 1527 his Spanish troops, reinforced by a large contingent of Germans, were headed south on the Italian boot toward Rome. His desperate Holiness signed another treaty with the Spanish ambassador, promising to pay tribute, but it was not only too little but too late. On May 6 the polyglot troops entered Rome. Before the month was out the city had been totally pillaged, and so many corpses had been thrown into the Tiber and left to rot in the streets that, with the coming of the summer heat, most of the invaders were driven out by plague. The Holy Father remained pent up in his castle until October, when he emerged to sign another treaty leaving the Papal States in his possession on condition that he give up geopolitics and call a council to reform the Church. He did neither (popes generally dreading councils), but Charles apparently was tired of dealing with him any more than necessary, especially now that he was broke and powerless. Small wonder that His Holiness refused to annul the marriage of England's Henry VIII to Catherine of Aragon, the emperor's aunt.

* * *

The Reformation's cleansing effect on the papacy was a slow process, for habits so long ingrained are hard to break. (It is notable that most if not all of history's "good" popes were *reforming* popes, although some seemed more anxious about specks in foreign eyes than logs in Roman eyes.) The 1600s and 1700s saw a change in the papacy's seamier side from concupiscence and cupidity to conservatism and condemnation while its temporal power crumbled under attack from liberal Italian politics and its spiritual authority eroded under the impact of rational inquiry. As late as 1650 Innocent X let his widowed sister-in-law virtually run the papal court, handing out political and ecclesiastical plums to cooperative favorites, and as late as the 1720s Benedict XIII kept on as his chief adviser one Cardinal Coscia, who, according to a Catholic historian, "set a shocking example of avarice and venality." The turning point might be assigned to Urban VIII, who ladeled out enormous sums to his relatives, waged a costly and abortive war for thirty months against the duchy of Parma (exhausting Vatican resources), and in the 1630s presided over the condemnation and house arrest of Galileo for insisting that the earth circles the sun.

There were plenty of other condemnations before, during and after Urban's time. Condemnation in doctrinal questions is at bottom what Rome is all about, winnowing the wheat and getting rid of the chaff, burning it when practicable. Ripe for condemnation were all those rebellious sectarian ideas spawned by the Reformation, which was followed by the even greater impudence of the Enlightenment, that cornucopia of material for the Holy Inquisition and the Index of Forbidden Books. The spread of printing and of literacy made it ever more difficult, yet more imperative, to stamp out not only wild-eyed heresies but also pernicious notions like democracy, pluralism, freedom—all those sassy ideas which had collectively come to be called "Modernism."

Although the Papal States were wrested from Napoleonic talons at the Congress of Vienna and largely restored to the papacy in 1815, uneasy would lie the heads that wore the tiara. Although the uneasiness was nothing new, its source was no longer the rapacity of rival princes but was rather the liberal politics of rising Italian nationalism. This new, modern threat was more menacing than mere rapacity, for it was ideological and righteous (and self-righteous), without a shred of proper respect for the divine right of autocrats. Even within the Papal States the democratic infection was spreading, and the popes reacted like other princely holdovers from the Middle Ages and the Renaissance, adding a religious component to their determined resistance. This component took the form of condemnations issued against the rising tide of independent thinking, culminating in the later 1800s in a veritable paroxysm of anathematizing fervor.

Papal reactions at first were chiefly political. After the restoration of his realm Pius VII (1800–23) and his secretary of state ruled with an iron resolve that greatly promoted the growth of the Carbonari, a secret society dedicated to introducing "constitutional government" into Italian politics. The arrest and execution of the society's leaders under Leo XII (1823–29), the increased use of the Inquisition apparatus, the return of the ghetto system for Jews, the forbidding of newfangled health measures like vaccination, the reinvigoration of censorship, the closing of taverns to clergy, the prohibition of the waltz as sinful, and a general reign of terror swiftly dissipated the residue of sympathy that had accrued to Pius VII because of his shabby treatment by Napoleon and his stoic courage during his ordeal. In the condemnation department Leo limited himself to repeating papal strictures against secret societies such as the Freemasons—which generally were secret, of course, because such papal and governmental strictures could have dismayingly lethal consequences.

Leo's successor, Pius VIII (1829–30) lasted only twenty months —unfortunately, for he displayed some inklings of open-minded tolerance. (The radicals of the day, after all, were generally less radical than the framers of the U.S. Constitution.) His tolerance, such as it was, may have been limited to politics; in the area of ecumenism, it was he who issued the ukase against priests' blessing a "mixed marriage" unless the non-Catholic partner agreed to raise the children as Catholics (a stipulation no longer included, although the Catholic is urged to make every effort in that direction).

Gregory XVI (1831–46) lasted 180 months, approximately— and also unfortunately, for his autocratic intransigence solidified the Church's reputation for insensible despotism. When a conference of ambassadors to the Holy See suggested some mild political reforms to ease some of the tension under papal rule, His Holiness reacted with glacial indifference, preferring to call in both French and Austrian troops to maintain law and order in his domain more effectively than his own undisciplined and cordially hated militia. When the French priest-philosopher Lamennais and his fellow intellectuals urged that the Church accommodate itself to democracy, turning to the people and away from divinely rightful aristocracies, the Holy Father issued two searing encyclicals condemning such outrageous ideas. He found intolerable "that obnoxious freedom of opinion that rages far and wide, to the ruin of Church and State." Also condemned were "shameless science" and freedom of the press, which can "never be sufficiently accursed." Such is the tradition of more recent popes' Predecessors of Happy Memory.

Shortly before Gregory died, several uprisings in the papal realm were violently suppressed, with a reported 2000 subjects outlawed, exiled or imprisoned. Before becoming pope, Gregory had written a widely read book supporting the temporal power of the papacy, as well as papal infallibility. His reign was a fitting prelude to the much longer reign of Pius IX.

PIUS IX (1846-78)

A few churchmen were disturbed by the hard-nosed theocracy of Gregory & Co. Among them was a Cardinal Mastai-Ferretti, who as bishop of Spoleto and then of Imola did what he could to protect people from Rome and Rome from itself. His hasty election to the papacy in July 1846, despite strong conservative opposition, was a surprise to most and a shock to many. Within a month he amnestied all the Papal States' political prisoners and outcasts, and soon thereafter he embarked on a program of softening bureaucratic arteries, introducing constitutional government with lay participation (except for Jews, of course), establishing a relatively free press, and incidentally becoming an idol of the people, who among other things took to singing hymns of his praises composed by Rossini. Soon prayers were being offered in some monasteries and nunneries that the church be saved from damage by this dangerously liberal pope.

His effort to accommodate the inevitable was not necessarily too little, but it was definitely too late. Italy's participation in the turmoil of 1848, that year of revolution in Europe, was its republican revolt to unify the political fragments of centuries into a single nation—with Rome as its capital. Unification was essentially achieved by 1861, with King Victor Emmanuel ensconced in its temporary capital, Florence, while dreaming of Rome, which at the time was protected by French arms. Rome would not be his until the fall of 1870, when Italian troops made that city the capital of Italy for the first time in 1400 years, to great popular acclaim. The dispossessed pope, confined to the Vatican with a limited sovereignty (symbolized by such concessions as the Swiss Guard and the Vatican post office), refused the new Italian government's offer of an annuity as compensation for his loss of territory. That territory, he firmly believed, was essential to the pope's spiritual authority.

In a plebiscite held soon afterward, his former subjects approved the incorporation of the Papal States into the Italian nation by a rather lopsided 99%. His Holiness had long ago lost the support of his people. In 1848 he had remained neutral when Italian nationalists waged war to expel the military interlopers from "Catholic Austria." When the nationalists returned triumphant from the fray, they occupied the Papal States and declared a republic. In the last of history's many papal flights, His Holiness took off in disguise for the safety of Naples. There he sent out a call for foreign help to which France and Austria responded. France proved the more effective, ousting the republicans in July 1849 and ceremoniously handing the keys of the city of Rome to its restored pontifical prince. The ceremony was held in Naples, however, for popular resentment would keep the cautious pope from entering the city until April 1850. He returned an embittered, irascible reactionary, fully convinced that constitutional government and freedom of the press were inherently, incorrigibly evil. He had changed so dramatically in this respect that he was to become known among the disenchanted as Pius the Ninth II.

Spurning requests for a full restoration of his reforms, His Holiness turned his attention increasingly to foreign affairs, completing favorable treaties with Spain and Austria, and most especially to religious matters, issuing major condemnations of liberal writings, reorganizing the hierarchy, and particularly setting in motion a program of declaring the Virgin Mary to have been conceived without original sin. His poll of 600 bishops and theologians on whether to define the Immaculate Conception produced a satisfying response of 90% affirmative. In December 1854 he proclaimed the doctrine, adding a disciplinary paragraph that clearly indicated his opinion on papal infallibility: "Wherefore, if any shall presume (which may God forbid!) to think in their hearts anything contrary to this definition of Ours, let them realize and well know that they have been condemned by their own judgment, have suffered shipwreck concerning the faith, and have broken away from the unity of the Church; and that besides all this they subject themselves to the lawful penalties if they dare to signify, by word or in writing, or by any other external means, what they think in their hearts."

Ten years later, in December 1864, he issued his apodictic and apoplectic *Syllabus of Errors* in connection with an encyclical condemning modern heresies. Its eighty propositions heatedly excoriated such notions as freedom of philosophical and scientific studies from ecclesiastical supervision and correction, the right of a person to practice religion as conscience dictates, the right of a State to regulate Church affairs, any suggestion that Catholicism is not the one true church, the possibility that popes and councils may ever have exceeded their rightful powers or made mistakes in matters of faith or morals, any impropriety in the Church's use of physical force, any precedence of civil laws over Church laws, education independent of church authority, the separation of Church and State, refusal to obey "legitimate princes," freedom of worship, and any papal obligation to "come to terms with progress, liberalism, and modern civilization."

Comment need hardly be added. The *Syllabus* speaks for itself, quite forcefully, quite authoritatively, representing the condemnatory compulsion in full flower.

Five years later, in December 1869, the first Vatican Council convened to confirm the Holy Father's sensations of infallibility. It did so the following July by an overwhelming vote, decreeing that the pope, "when in discharge of the office of Pastor and Doctor [teacher] of all Christians . . . defines a doctrine regarding faith or morals to be held by the Universal Church . . . is possessed of that infallibility with which the divine Redeemer willed that his Church should be endowed for defining doctrine regarding faith or morals: and that therefore such definitions of the Roman Pontiff are irreformable of themselves, and not from the consent of the Church." Curiously, the definition is self-defeating: no pope has ever been "in discharge of the office of Pastor and Doctor of all Christians" unless "Christians" are limited to "persons accepting the authority of the Roman pope." This little flaw, however, does not seem to have interfered with the production of categorical assertions, in either the imperious giving or the pusillanimous receiving.

The definition was promulgated, with the customary curse of anathema for dissenters, in the summer of 1870. Although the council was not formally adjourned, it was effectively ended by the republicans' capture of Rome and the pope's retreat into the Vatican. This time his appeals to foreigners for armed rescue went unheeded. But he did have the satisfaction of excommunicating all those involved, directly or indirectly, in the seizure of his domain. For they had engaged, in his view, in a conflict "between Christ and Belial, between light and darkness, between truth and lies, between justice and usurpation." In short, between black and white. He seemed to find some recompense in natural disasters (earthquakes, floods) visited upon a guilty Italy by an avenging Jesus. He would spend his last eight years in self-imposed imprisonment in the Vatican, supported largely by worldwide Peter's Pence collections and hoping vainly for a divinely inspired restoration of his kingdom. "Relief," he had said, "must come from heaven."

LEO XIII (1878-1903)

Relief did not come from heaven or from anywhere else. Confinement to the Vatican, however voluntary, did nothing to broaden papal outlooks. Pius' successor, Leo XIII, despite his later reputation as a liberal pope, was as fully devoted to papal prerogatives, though less angrily and not so single-mindedly. As one of the curial architects of the *Syllabus* and the infallibility doctrine, he continued the feverish Indexing of books and pamphlets that advocated coming to terms with the modern world. He did relax to the extent of favoring the separation of Church and State— but in non-Catholic countries. He was interested in promoting historical scholarship, even when it uncovered unwelcome facts, but in the teaching of philosophy he decreed a tyranny of neo-Thomism. His famous encyclical on the rights of labor followed one condemning socialism and was followed by another condemning "Americanism" as an unwarranted compromise with secular society. He encouraged Catholics in France to cooperate with the republican government while forbidding Italian Catholics even to vote. He made overtures to the Anglicans but issued a bull declaring their ordinations invalid. A bit of a papal Proteus, he.

He was certainly no flaming radical. His view of Catholicism rings rather clearly in counsel that he addressed to members of a Catholic workers' association, urging them to "submit all your projects and works to the pastors of the churches whom you wish to have as presidents. It is, in fact, divinely ordained by the church that it is the right and duty of the bishops to dictate the rules and to march at the head through doctrine and example, while it is part of the faithful to follow in the footsteps of the pastors, to obey their precepts with docility and to express their filial love to them while generously offering them their practical assistance."

Although his basic premises were those of Pius IX, he presented them more gently. Early in his reign the body of Pius was transferred to its final resting place, and during the funeral procession the coffin was pelted with stones and at one point was in danger of being tossed into the Tiber by an angry mob. Leo's funeral procession experienced no such indignities.

PIUS X (1903–14)

Leo's record of sporadic, selective accommodation did not last long. The accession of Cardinal Guiseppi Sarto, Patriarch of Venice, to the papacy, in the words of papal biographer Carlo Falconi, "signified neither more or less than a return to the latter days of Pius IX, when, after fulminating anathemas against progress and civilization, he had immured himself in the Vatican as in a fortress to ensure the Church's survival. It was as if the whole pontificate of Leo XIII, who had brought the Church back into the world and a large part of the world back into the Church, had never existed." This may sound too hard on both Piuses, and well as too easy on Leo, but the record speaks for itself. St. Pius X may be the most recent example of how a personally upright, kindly individual can be a disastrous pope.

The contrast between the personalities of the aloof, patrician, protocol-conscious Leo and his plebeian, cordial, old-shoe successor was enough to remind one today of Dorothy Parker's comparison of the Grecian urn with the mess of pottage. The contrast would prove even greater in the conduct of the papacy. As Patriarch of Venice Sarto had offered a foretaste when he banned Catholic attendance at the city's first Art Exhibition because he considered one of the paintings antireligious. One of his first acts as pope was to rid church music of all such modern secular distortions as had been provided by composers like Verdi and Rossini, returning it to the pristine chant of the Middle Ages. Another was to launch a thorough codification of canon law, a project whose 2414 articles would introduce a heavy pall of legalism on the Church.

An incident involving the Swiss Guard was illustrative. It was a Vatican custom for a new pope to grant the guardsmen a gratuity in addition to their pay, but the financially strapped Leo had not done so; a threat of mutiny, however, quickly changed his mind. Pius likewise announced that there would be no gratuity; a threat of mutiny merely brought a decree dissolving the guard. After much pleading, even from Switzerland, he relented, and the guardsmen were reinstated, sans gratuity.

The bugaboo of his papacy was Modernism, especially "scientific Modernism." To rid the Church of its taint he vigorously employed the Supreme Congregation of the Holy Office (the Inquisition), the Sacred Congregation of the Index, the Consistorial Congregation (with its friendly visits to suspect dioceses) and, after 1908, his secretary of state's secret police. Contemporary accounts by friend and foe give a picture resembling that of the early 1950s in the United States, clouded with the petty hatreds of the inquisitorial committees led by Joseph R. McCarthy and J. Parnell Thomas. What Communism was to McCarthy and Thomas, as well as to the pope of their time, Modernism was to Pius X. Others might read Modernist writings with some equanimity, he once commented, "but I read what is concealed between the lines, and there I find errors." The errors, arising in his view out of a satanic hostility to Catholic Truth, represented a deadly peril. To an archbishop who had protested against Roman oppression he wrote, "I am surprised that you consider excessive those measures taken to restrict the flood threatening to swamp us when the error that they are trying to disseminate is much deadlier than Luther's, since it is pointedly aimed at destroying not merely the Church but Christianity." "They" were not insidious infidels but were Catholics, mostly clerical and lay theologians and philosophers, who were worried over Rome's alienation not only of intellectuals but also of the intelligent through its rejection of rational inquiry and modern scholarship.

His Holiness took to calling "them" Modernists (including others denounced by Pius IX) because of their efforts to modernize Roman doctrine, to make it more compatible with developments in scientific, political and social thinking. Just what the controversy was all about has grown rather vague over the intervening decades, clouded as it was by intemperate wrangling. What does seem fairly clear is that some of the Modernists slipped into heresy, denying any divinity in Christ for example, and often stating their beliefs in the dogmatically absolute terms of the obsessive controversialist. Someone given to reading between the lines could find plenty to condemn without half trying, and that is what His Holiness did, tarring moderation and extremism with one broad brush in the tradition of the *Syllabus of Errors*. Thus the scholars who questioned the literal historicity of the Bible and the polemicist who denied creation, the student who questioned the subordination of State to Church and the radical who condemned all institutional religion, the doubtful thinker and the fanatic debater, all found themselves pretty much under the same anathema. Rome in its paranoia was not entertaining fine distinctions.

And so the 65 viewpoints condemned by the new syllabus of 1907 included the notions that Church teaching should be affected by scriptural scholarship, that at least some human knowledge is independent of Church (Rome's) authority, that the Church (Rome) is unreasonable in trying to exercise thought control (demanding "internal assent"), that dogmas are less than revealed truth. Feel as we do or be damned, this was Rome's overriding shibboleth, an attitude hardly likely to invite intellectual respectability. What it did invite, indeed, beyond the adoring submission of the incorrigibly committed, was indifference and ridicule. Nor was this reaction likely to be mitigated by the title of the Holy Father's encyclical that did the wholesale condemning. It was "Feeding the Flock of the Lord."

The loss of intellectual vigor in the Church was immense.

Even in the United States, where Modernism was so inchoate that no American theological writing was Indexed, the atmosphere was oppressive, according to *The Catholic Encyclopedia,* which describes it as "the stifling of scriptural studies in the United States. Seminary faculties were carefully reviewed and devoted themselves to training pastors. Bishops were chosen for their complete orthodoxy. The ordinary clergyman hesitated to say anything theological, and the layman lapsed into complete silence on religious matters." An ideal situation, no doubt, in the view of John Paul & Co.: the Good Old Days.

BENEDICT XV (1914–22)

While still a cardinal, Bologna's Archbishop Giacomo Della Chiesa had been accused of unorthodoxy by the "Integralists," Pius' most heated supporters of papal tyranny. An aristocrat like Leo, he was, as Pope Benedict XV, capable of a sophisticated tolerance quite foreign to minds like those of the two Piuses. His resemblance to Leo, in contrast with Pius X, evidently influenced his election, for Europe was already at war and many cardinals felt that a conciliatory attitude would be much more likely to calm things down than would a siege mentality. Surely this was true, but Benedict's valiant efforts to shorten the war and soften the peace terms could not overcome his predecessor's legacy of widespread contempt.

His conciliatory attitude found expression in the improvement, indeed the reestablishment, of civil relationships with the governments of France, despite that country's thoroughgoing separation of Church and State, and of Italy, despite his private conviction of his right to the Papal States, or at least to papal states.

It was expressed also in his handling of the Modernist controversy. He obviously could not contradict his immediate Predecessor of Happy Memory, and he surely had no wish to undermine papal authority. In his first encyclical he referred to Pius' lashing of Modernism: "We hereby renew that condemnation in all its fullness." He also asserted papal authority: "Let all know to whom God has entrusted the office of the Church's teacher, and leave the field free for him so that he may speak as and when he sees fit." Yet he conceded that there were still some topics on which Rome had not yet spoken, and on these, "in due faith and discipline . . . it is certainly permitted to everyone to give and maintain his [though perhaps not her] own opinion." Give it, that is, in a low voice and with courtesy: "But in such discussions let everyone refrain from excess in speech . . . and let him not accuse others of suspect faith or lack of discipline for the simple reason that they hold different views from his own." Such a viewpoint must have created some alarm, and perhaps even some apoplexy, in curial quarters, yet probably not so much as his consolidating the Congregation of the Index into the Congregation of the Holy Office, suggesting that one agency of inquisition would do for the 20th century. During his eight-year reign only ten books were put on the Index.

He died at the age of 67, a young man by modern papal standards. During most of his brief tenure he was agonizingly preoccupied with the horrors of the war. A longer, more peaceful reign might have enabled him to drag the Church into the 19th century, if not the 20th. But while he lasted he was, relatively at least, a breath of fresh air.

PIUS XI (1922–39)

The air grew somewhat staler during the reign of his successor, a 65-year-old middle-class professional librarian, the only librarian ever to occupy the pontifical throne. After 30 years in libraries, including four years as head of the Vatican Library, in 1919 he was appointed papal delegate to Poland, where he spent a couple of years acquiring an intense distaste for Russian Communism and a tolerance for dictatorship as exemplified by the redoubtable Marshall Pilsudski. In March 1921 he was appointed archbishop of Milan, and less than twelve months later he was pope.

In the rise of Benito Mussolini he saw an opportunity to arrange a concordat that would restore enough real estate to the papacy to assure its sovereignty more fully. There was no hope of making such an arrangement with the Italian republicans, tinged as they were with chronic anticlericalism. But Mussolini was much more accommodating. Early in 1929, soon after he had ended parliamentary democracy in Italy, he concluded a concordat with the Holy Father ceding about 109 acres of the city of Rome to papal sovereignty, settled financial claims for a stupendous 1.75 billion lire (providing the wherewithal for a frenzy of building and art patronage worthy of Renaissance days), and declared Catholicism the official state religion. Within two years, however, relations became strained when restrictions began to be imposed on the official religion. Similarly with Adolf Hitler, His Holiness lost his concordat enthusiasm after he began to realize that here was something more than a simple anti-Communist. This was not the case with Francisco Franco, who remained reasonably accommodating to the Church even over the long term.

Of his thirty encyclicals one of the best known is *Quadra-gessimo Anno,* condemning the evils of a "hard, cruel and relentless" capitalism but warning against an "impious and nefarious" Communism or an irreligious socialism as alternatives and recommending more equitable distribution of national income, with profit sharing and worker participation in management (as usual, without recommending any means to such ends). He encouraged lay activity, particularly the Catholic Action movement, which he called "the organized participation of the laity in the hierarchical apostate," conducted of course under Proper Supervision. He generally did not see Red where there was none, at least in cases involving personalities: when a French bishop donated money to a strike fund and was eagerly reported to Rome as a Marxist, he was made a cardinal. When a violently worded attack on secularism was issued by the French bishops, many if not most of whom had been appointed by Pius IX, he dissociated himself from it. Eventually he condemned the writings of the Catholic radical right in France, to the astonished consternation of many a French and Roman prelate.

Some of his encyclicals were rather sophisticated, others were not: "Today, as We see you threatened with new dangers and molestations, We say to you that if anyone preaches to you a gospel other than the one you received on the knees of a pious mother, from the lips of a believing father . . . let him be anathema." One such impious gospel was that of Communism, which in the Soviet Union was not content with being merely agnostic but had to be militantly atheistic: although the Vatican

Mission in 1922 saved thousands of Russians from starvation, in 1923 an official Communist Party circular described religion as "an evil no less pernicious than alcoholism or prostitution." With its economic tunnel vision, Marxism could see religion as nothing more than a pillar of unjust society, and to extirpate it the bolsheviks launched persecutions rivaling if not outdoing those of pagan Rome. By 1937 His Holiness vented his anger, horror and frustration in an encyclical: "Communism is intrinsically wrong and no one who would save Christian civilization may collaborate with it in any undertaking whatsoever." This extreme, absolute condemnation would prove to be a baton to pass on to his successor, in both senses of the term. It would set the stage on which Catholicism would be accused, by no means unjustifiably, as being little more than "incensed" anti-Communism—in both senses of *that* term.

Another encyclical would set another stage. By 1930 technology had brought artificial contraception within the fairly easy reach of Mr. and Mrs. John O'Doe, to the vast alarm of Rome's professional celibates. Not only does uninhibited spawning greatly enhance Catholicism's quantitative dimensions (today Latin Americans constitute nearly half the world's nominal Catholics), but sexual pleasure must have its price, and the price must be paid. And so the end of that year saw the publication of a celebrated encyclical condemning every artificial means of birth control as a "criminal abuse" and gravely sinful—again, "intrinsically," because "the conjugal act is destined primarily by nature for the begetting of children." (If this conduct is "criminal abuse," what language is left for, say, rape or sexual child abuse?) For good measure, the ukase added condemnations of every artificial abortion ("Thou shalt not kill") and every divorce ("What God has joined together let no man put asunder").

The encyclical, like other pontifical dicta, rested on unsupported assertions (does God's word need any underpinning?) couched in sentimental verbiage comprising pious ambiguities and nonsequiturs: each marriage, it informed the bleating faithful for instance, arises out of the spouses' free consent, "and this free act of the will, by which each party hands over and accepts those rights proper to the state of marriage, is so necessary to constitute true marriage that it cannot be supplied by any human power." Recently a prominent American Catholic bishop in a television interview with David Brinkley responded to a question about likely Catholic lay nonconformance with Rome's "Instruction" condemning all artificial insemination by saying that the Church (i.e., Rome) has to do a better job of explaining its positions. He did not mention reasoned argument, leaving his viewers to guess why.

At the end of his 17-year reign the Holy Father was reluctant to leave the "mighty drama" of the world. His view of it was simple, that of the spiritual autocrat: "God and evil are locked in a titanic struggle. No one in these times has the right to remain indifferent." And the fewer distinctions, the better.

PIUS XII (1939–58)

With the coronation of Eugene Pacelli, 63, the papacy was again in the hands of an Italian aristocrat. Intelligent, literate, cultured, with valuable experience as his predecessor's secretary of state, Pius XII was doubtless the obvious choice for the cardinals to make, what with the world on the brink of a catastrophic war. Catholics—episcopal, clerical and lay—would be among the enthusiasts on both sides: the Holy Father's conduct of papal diplomacy has become a subject for controversy, courageously adroit or cravenly insensitive, depending on one's viewpoint. He accepted, for instance, a personal representative from the President of the United States, disapproved (though silently) of Italy's entry into the war, and rescued thousands of Jews, but after Hitler's attack on the citadel of atheistic Communism he praised the Axis armies, in a radio speech, as engaged in "magnanimous acts of valor which now defend the foundations of Christian culture." Like Benedict XV, he was ignored in the making of the peace.

After the war he continued the policy of intransigent hostility to Communism, decreeing excommunication in 1949 for any Catholic who voted for or otherwise supported Communists, a decree apparently as much honored in the breach as in the observance. In 1952–53 he even tried, through the activity of the Catholic Action organization, to ally Italy's Christian Democratic party with the neo-Fascists.

His anti-Communism was so obsessive that biographers have taken to explaining it in psychological terms. Some trace it at least partly to an unpleasant experience he had as papal legate in Munich. In March 1919, during a worker's rebellion, a band of armed Communist revolutionaries forced their way into the legation in a very unfriendly way. Archbishop Pacelli, facing them coolly and defiantly on the stairs to the upper floor, demanded that they cease their violation of the legation's extraterritorial sovereignty and leave at once. After a tense moment of confused hesitancy, they did so. But the incident was so shocking to Pacelli's sensitive nature that he often had bad dreams about it for the rest of his life.

Communism, he maintained, was based on Darwin's notion of human evolution, which he dismissed as unproven speculation (in a notorious August 1950 encyclical, *Humani Generis,* "Concerning Certain False Opinions"). False opinions must be "cured" by "Catholic theologians and philosophers [who] have a grave responsibility for defending truth, both human and divine, and for installing it in men's minds." Human reason "must be trained on the right principles [of] that sound philosophy which we have long possessed as an heirloom [from] former ages of Christendom." For where the "all-important questions are concerned, what progress is possible?" Progress is possible only in divinely guided elaborations of divinely established truth, and this is the exclusive function of Rome, appointed as "the Living Teacher to illustrate and develop those truths which are contained only obscurely and as it were by implication in the storehouse of faith." Such an assertion opens the way for unsupported conjectures such as no respectable evolutionist would tolerate, and a couple of months later His Holiness proclaimed the dogma of Mary's bodily assumption into heaven.

Mary, though a mother, was a virgin. The virgin state is (must therefore be?) superior to the married state because its purpose is "to aim only at the divine, to turn thereto the whole mind and soul; to want to please God in everything, to think of Him continually, to consecrate body and soul completely to Him." His Holiness knew this because St. Paul wrote that a married person "is solicitous for the things of this world" (a remark made under divine inspiration, a state yet to be defined) and because St. Thomas, the "Angelic Doctor," wrote that marriage "keeps the soul from abandonment to God's service." How this kind of skyhook deductive thinking fits with the data of experience required for inductive thinking is something about which people acquainted with professional celibates can give evidence.

Some Church historians writing during the reign of this pope's successor, grown heady with "aggiornamento" (the ecclesiastical buzzword for modernization), spoke of the passing of Pius XII as the end of an era. Little did they know.

JOHN XXIII (1958–63)

Karl Otmar von Aretin's *The Papacy and the Modern World* contains a photograph of Pius XII and Cardinal Angelo Roncalli, the future John XXIII, and the contrast between the two men is little short of comical. (John XXIII is included here, among the "embarrassing" popes, because he was so differently embarrassing, especially to rigid conservatives.) There stands Pius, tall and thin, militarily erect, staring rigidly ahead, his face set in stern preoccupation, his hands clasped tightly before him. Beside him stands Roncalli, short and round, rather slumping, beaming at the camera, his face soft with a friendly smile, his hands clasped loosely and resting on his gently protuberant belly.

This humble friendliness was a good omen, as was the fact that as a young priest he had been denounced by the Holy Office for his friendliness with Modernists. As Patriarch of Venice he had actually granted an audience to delegates from an organization not only of Communists, but of Communist *women!* His early years as pope, however, were at best ambiguous. His election, indeed, had pleased both curial standpatters and foreign cardinal modernizers. Whatever doubts may have occurred to either group faded before the conviction that this pope was likely to be no more than an inconsequential transition. But then in January 1959, only three months after his election, he offered a shocker: in a very informal meeting of such curial cardinals as he could round up he briefly announced his main projects: to call an ecumenical council to promote Christian unity, to hold a synod on Roman problems, and to start a reform of canon law. And immediately the curial cardinals began thinking about damage control.

They seem to have been pretty successful. The Roman synod was held and canon laws were shifted about without causing the bureaucracy more than some minor discomfort. As for the second Vatican Council, despite the delight with which it was welcomed by liberal Catholics, it would wind up mired in garrulous ambiguity, subject to interpretation by powers that be. Even if John had lived longer, the results might not have been any clearer (one of his heroes was Pius IX). His death, and his successor, guaranteed that they wouldn't be.

PAUL VI (1963–78)

Giovanni Montini, as Paul VI, seems to have been a man well fitted to carry on a tradition of ambiguity. A good friend of Pope John, whose work he promised to continue, he was a much more intimate associate of Pius XII, with whom and for whom he worked in the secretariat of state for 30 years. He created new cardinals to internationalize the curia without changing it very much. He set a retirement age for bishops at 75 and for cardinals at 80, and as pope spoke of his death, diffidently, as a "providential solution" that would allow his successor to be more effective, yet he reached his 80th birthday without a hint of his own resignation. He reiterated his predecessors' condemnation of Communism but ignored their injunctions against dealing with Communists and wrote a social encyclical that *The Wall Street Journal* decried as "souped-up Marxism." He deplored the shortage of priests but forbade any relaxation of clerical celibacy. He abolished the Index of Forbidden Books but not the star-chamber ambience of curial inquisitions. He expressed concern over the world's population explosion, as in Latin America, but in 1968, in his still reverberating encyclical *Humanae Vitae,* condemned all artificial birth control as gravely sinful.

That encyclical has overshadowed his papacy. It is what he is remembered for, not only because of its message but also because of the controversy that preceded it and especially the controversy that has followed it. He anticipated the latter: a couple of months after its publication he intoned a papal supplication, "May the lively debate aroused by Our encyclical lead to a better understanding of God's will." His sincerity here may be open to question (his present successor is certainly no lover of lively debate), but not his foresight, for the debate's liveliness, and its durability, have proved even greater than anything he could have had in mind. Indeed, he probably would have agreed with the Brazilian cab driver in a story relayed by William Shannon in *The Lively Debate:* when the cabbie was told that the pope had banned the pill, he replied, "They should never have told him about it."

The pill was what it was all about. It was unknown when Pius XI forbade contraception in 1930, but by the early 1960s its use had grown so phenomenally that Rome felt compelled to extend the prohibition to include it. Like Pius & Co., Paul & Co. were constrained to derive their condemnation from an interpretation of "the natural law," since former condemnations, based on an interpretation of the sin of Onan in Genesis (38:9) had been discredited by 19th-century Biblical scholarship. (Onan's sin was not in "spilling his seed" but in failing to copulate with his brother's widow genuinely in order to give her children, thereby breaking Jewish law.) Early in the encyclical, issued in July 1968, Rome's right "to interpret the natural moral law" was asserted as "in fact indisputable" because of Christ's commission "to Peter and the other Apostles . . . to teach all nations His command-ments." The inclusion of "the other Apostles" received no emphasis.

After a nod of restrained approval to the rhythm method, a warning was issued on the consequences of contraception, such as increased extramarital sex, lower moral standards, and state intrusion into the bedroom. This presumably was meant as an argument but was later implicitly described as irrelevant in a passage addressed to priests, who were instructed "to give an example of that sincere obedience which is due the magisterium of the Church [i.e., Rome]. For, as you know, the pastors of the Church [in the Vatican] enjoy a special light of the Holy Spirit in teaching the truth. And this, rather than the arguments they put forward, is why you are bound to such obedience."

Rome having spoken, the case is closed.

The lack of confidence in the arguments may have been inspired (if that's the appropriate word in this context) by the overwhelming majority opinion of the papal commission appointed earlier to lay the groundwork for the encyclical. Although instructed by Paul & Co. to condemn contraception, the commission decided after two years of study and debate that *marriage,* not the individual sex act, must be open to procreation and that Rome's earlier condemnations of contraception (like its still earlier disapproval of any sexual pleasure in marriage) were not unalterable. Even the minority members concluded that contraception could not be considered immoral on the basis of natural law. Paul & Co.'s response to the commission's effort, to put it in an American vernacular, was "What do *they* know?"

The commission's conclusion, offered in a 12-volume report, preceded the encyclical by two years, during which the inevitable leaks prepared Catholics at all levels for a relaxing of Rome's attitude toward contraception. It also prepared them to react to the encyclical's rigidity with shocked protest. Rome, evidently nervous about this possibility, preceded its publication with a letter to all bishops from the papal secretary of state urging them to close ranks behind it and "to explain and justify the reasons for it" to the uncomprehending faithful. The bishops' reaction was to refuse to parrot, but not to refuse to weasel.

The reaction was varied, roughly dividing the bishops into three groups, one totally supportive, another wavering between loyalty to the pope and sympathetic concern for their married people, and a third showing that concern by conceding a lay couple's right to follow their consciences. Some of the bishops suggested that no serious sin was involved: although the catechism distinction between "mortal" and "venial" sin was not mentioned, and although the encyclical had indicated that erring couples should rely on confession and communion for forgiveness and strength, the Austrian bishops explicitly advised them that they could legitimately "receive Holy Communion without first going to confession." All in all, it was hardly the kind of automatic saluting that Rome had requested.

Theologians were similarly divided. More than 600 Americans signed a strong contradictory statement: "As Roman Catholic theologians, conscious of our duty and our limitations, we conclude that spouses may responsibly decide according to their conscience that artificial contraception in some circumstances is permissible and indeed necessary to preserve and foster the values and the sacredness of marriage." Others saluted as ordered. Between the two groups reactions ranged from teeth-clenching to shoulder-shrugging, while most of the laity, suspended between infallible irrationality and fallible sanity, did pretty much as they pleased. Ten years later, according to a survey conducted by the sociologiost-priest Andrew Greeley, 87% of American Catholics disagreed with the encyclical. In a way, Rome has been hoist on its own petard, for it has traditionally accepted supremacy of conscience—everyone is morally obliged to follow his or her own conscience—although the curialists hasten to add that it must be a *right* conscience.

* * *

In Church history, Rome has been wrong and immoral often

enough not to put on airs. While it has occupied itself with such matters as princely competitions, family rivalries, property acquisition and retention, and the evils of science, sex and human freedom, the Church as a whole seems to have been borne through the ages by the people who make it up. The Holy Spirit seems to have saved the Church sometimes through the papacy, and sometimes from it. Rome, given its spotty, and spotted, record, could at least show a little more diffidence.

Other Popes, Other Mavericks

If Rome's present affirmations of degrees of infallibility mean that a teaching can be infallible enough to have a "binding" moral authority, and if this claim is justified by reference to papal tradition, then surely it is worthwhile to refer to that tradition. Although the vast majority of papal declarations are unverifiable and undeniable because they deal with transubstantial mysteries like the Eucharist and skyhook assumptions like the Assumption, a few can be checked against gritty reality because popes have occasionally pontificated impulsively and indiscreetly. In such cases they have been contradicted by gritty reality, gritty successors, or both. Yet they have not been the victims. The victims have been the mavericks who had to wait for years or centuries to be exonerated.

The most famous case of such victimization is that of Galileo Galilei. Familiar though it is, it could hardly be omitted here. It has been described often enough as not involving absolute papal infallibility. Yet the degree of papal infallibility involved was at least as high as that involved in recent declarations against contraception, for the condemnation of Galileo was based on Rome's authority to interpret scripture, not merely the natural law.

URBAN VIII AND GALILEO (1564-1642)

One evening Galileo Galilei, the Duke of Tuscany's resident mathematician and philosopher, attended one of the lavish dinners which the duke often gave in Florence for local celebrities. During dinner a debate arose over why objects in water float or sink. The conservatives at the table reverently cited the Aristotelian dogma that it all depended on their shape. Galileo, ever disputatious, countered with the Archimedean explanation that it all depended on whether the water displaced weighed less or more than the object. This eminently verifiable inductive explanation enraged the Aristotelians, but Galileo stuck to his guns and in so doing received the support of another guest, a cardinal named Maffeo Barberini. As a result the two men became good friends, although a quarter of a century later Barberini, as Pope Urban VIII, would have Galileo arrested for impiously asserting that the earth moves around the sun.

Galileo was not readily disposed to accept arbitrary authority as a fount of knowledge. Less than two years earlier, having studied the moon through his newfangled telescope, he had openly written that he had found its surface "uneven, rough and full of cavities and prominences, being not unlike the face of the earth, relieved by chains of mountains and deep valleys." Some of the mountains he estimated to be as much as 20,000 feet high, with remarkable accuracy. All this flew in the scowling

faces of the Arisotelians, who earned their daily bread by promul-
gating the Divine Philosopher's notions, in this case the dictum
that heavenly bodies, including and indeed especially the moon,
were made of a mysteriously unearthly, perfect and incorruptible
substance that could never tolerate such imperfections as cavities
and prominences. A little later, after discovering the four major
moons of Jupiter, Galileo reported on these planetary anomalies,
on the solar blemishes we now call sunspots, and on the lunar
imperfections, all in a little book, *The Starry Messenger*. This
book, especially in also reporting on the moon-like phases of
Venus, put him quite firmly in the Copernican camp of central
sun and revolving planets. Aristotelians, Catholic and Protestant
(Luther and Melancthon were rigidly anti-Copernican), fussed
and fumed in a welter of deductive polemic, but without much
effect. Not until a stern academic named Lodovico Colombe
introduced scripture into the controversy did the dark clouds
of alleged impiety appear on the horizon.

In the spring of 1611 Galileo visited Rome, where he was
feted and lionized, elected to a prestigious scientific academy,
and granted a friendly audience with Pope Paul V. He was a
celebrity now, attracting attention both welcome and unwelcome:
a high profile in the ecclesiastical atmosphere of the time could
be as hazardous to one's health as it can be today in, say, the
Soviet Union. His considerable talent for ridicule exacerbated
the apprehensive hostility that his ideas provoked, making his
profile not only high but irresistible as a target. Further aggravation arose out of his weakness for the flat assertion; he was
often warned by his anxious friend Cardinal Robert Bellarmine,
among others, that he would be wiser to present his heliocentrism

as hypothesis rather than established fact.

By December 1613 scripture must have become a major element in the controversy, for at that time Galileo wrote a long letter to a friend explaining his very modern view of its proper function in the accumulation of knowledge. He was not contradicting scripture, he argued, for, "although scripture cannot err, its expositors and interpreters are in many ways liable to error, and one error especially would be very grave and frequent if we always stopped at the literal meaning." Such literal interpretation would reveal many contradictions, incorporate heresies and blasphemies, and make it "necessary to give God hands and feet and ears, and human and bodily emotions such as anger, repentance, hatred and sometimes forgetfulness of past events." Given that scripture can be wrongly interpreted, "I think that it would be prudent if men were forbidden to use passages of scripture to maintain that which our senses or demonstrated proof may show to be the contrary." Scripture, he insisted, teaches us faith and morality, not astronomy.

Such a view was anathema to many, among them a Dominican priest named Lorini, who reported to the Holy Office of the Inquisition that Galileo's "letter contains many propositions that seem suspect or presumptuous, as when it maintains that the language of holy scripture does not mean what it seems to mean, that in discussing natural phenomena the last and lowest place should be assigned to the authority of the sacred text, that its commentators have very often been mistaken in their interpretation, that the holy scripture should not be concerned with any but religious matters," and so on. At about the same time another Dominican, named Cacini, began a reverberating crusade against Copernican astronomy, citing the famous passage in Joshua 10 that describes the sun and moon standing still in the valley of Ajalon "until the nation took revenge on its enemies." He put so many eggs in this basket that even his Dominican superiors were embarrassed enough to apologize to Galileo. Cardinal Bellarmine, however, came to Cacini's aid by citing Solomon's divinely inspired description of the sun rising, setting, and returning "to its place."

The scriptural aspect of the burgeoning debate seemed to be getting stickier by the minute. In 1615 Cacini, tireless in pursuit, hied himself to Rome for a personal, formal denunciation of Galileo before the Inquisition. Galileo, although ill, also went to Rome to defend himself. But early in 1616, after consulting eleven theologians but no scientists, the inquisitorial cardinals condemned heliocentrism and the notion that the earth rotates (much less revolves) as contrary to scripture and therefore heretical—and filed their report away for the next 17 years. For the time being Galileo was told, as Cardinal Bellarmine put it in a kind of deposition that was meant to be helpful, that heliocentrism "is contrary to the holy scriptures and therefore must not be defended or held." (Galileo interpreted this as allowing him to *think* heliocentrism.) Even the Jesuits, generally sympathetic to his ideas at least as individuals, were peremptorily silenced by their Superior General, presumably on orders from the pope. When the duke called Galileo back to Florence, the muzzled astronomer was not unhappy to leave the papal city.

But he returned there in 1624, having dedicated a book, *The Assayer,* to the recently elected Pope Urban VIII, his old friend Barberini. The two men had several long, cordial conversations, yet His Holiness would not revoke the scripturally orthodox condemnation of 1616. The following year, back in Florence, Galileo began work on his most famous treatise, *Dialogue Concerning the Two Great World Systems, Ptolemaic and Copernican.* (It was chiefly the second-century Alexandrian Ptolemy who had fastened Aristotle on medieval astronomy.) Often ill, he worked slowly and sporadically, and it was not until February 1632 that the book was published, after approval by a rashly sympathetic censor. That October he was ordered to come to Rome to appear before the Inquisition for a little chat. Despite his illness and opportunities to escape to Switzerland or take refuge in Venice, he arrived in Rome in February 1633, and his interrogation began in April. During the three-month ordeal he was kept not in the customary prison but rather under fairly comfortable house arrest: his age, illness, reputation, and papal friendship apparently saved him from the usual common-criminal treatment. Because the book had presented his adversaries' arguments as coming from a simpleton, and because the pope thought he detected an unflattering resemblance to his pontifical self, the prisoner could expect no substantial rescue from an embittered Urban, who in any case was preoccupied with acquisitive nepotism, architectural extravagance, and Machiavellian politics.

After about three months of sporadic badgering, the exhausted pioneer broke down and recanted, even to the humiliating point of promising to denounce "any heretic or person suspected of heresy." Utterly defeated, thoroughly depressed, he was placed under continued house arrest for the remaining nine years of his life. During his last four years he was blind, though never

so blind as his behind-the-scenes antagonist, the avaricious, scheming, vindictive Holy Father who had allowed Rome's nearly
infallible, almost irreformable, relatively absolute teaching authority to invite the ridicule of intelligent people with simple instru-
ments to operate and eyes to see.

INNOCENT XI AND RICHARD SIMON (1638-1712)

It was humanly inevitable that the spirit of rational inquiry which
had motivated Galileo would motivate others to shed its unflattering light on religious beliefs. Galileo himself, in his defense
against the charge of contradicting scripture, had argued that
the Bible should not be imposed as a divinely dictated scientific
encyclopedia but rather should be taken as a divinely authoritative
guide only on matters of faith and morals. Within half a century
after his death pious doctrines were being zealously scrutinized
by thinkers and scribblers of the emerging Enlightenment, among
them Descartes, Pascal, Spinoza—and Richard Simon, a Catholic
priest and scholar from Normandy, in the France of His Mag-
nificence, Louis XIV.

Simon's specialty was Bible study based on historical research.
To pursue this study he learned not only Greek and Latin but
also Hebrew, Aramaic and other languages of Biblical times.
Although historical data were being used increasingly in the study
of secular texts (with the possible exception of the works of
the divine Aristotle—it was then a violation of French law to
contradict him), the sacred scriptures were quite another matter.
As a result of such independence of mind, as well as the inability
to suffer foolishness gladly, Simon was regularly embroiled in

controversy with other members of his Oratorian order, with Sorbonne academics, with Benedictines, with Jesuits, with his politically powerful bishop Jacques Bossuet, and ultimately with Rome under Pope Innocent XI. Further aggravation was provided by his distaste for the cloying "devotions" encrusting the liturgy and his contempt for official anti-Semitism: on one occasion, by submitting a kind of friend-of-the-court brief, he saved three hapless Jews from the stake.

His *Critical History of the Old Testament,* published in 1678 in response to an attack by Spinoza on Biblical inspiration, included historical observations on the doubtfulness of the authorship of some Biblical books (Moses, Matthew), the common use of the "son of man" in Aramaic, and the common partaking of ceremonial meals like the Last Supper, all generally accepted today. Bishop Bossuet, informed of such peripheral content, managed to have the censor's approval withdrawn, and then ordered copies of the book confiscated and fed to truth-protecting flames. Rome cooperated by placing Simon's works on the Index. Expelled from his order, Simon was relegated to a small parish in Normandy. Meanwhile several editions of the *Critical History,* published in Holland, found a multitude of eager readers.

In 1689 he added to the Index with a similarly critical history of the *New* Testament, and in 1702 with a New Testament translation, impertinently unauthorized. He continued writing until his death in 1712. Although his scholarship was often flawed by modern standards, his general approach has been thoroughly vindicated, and today he is widely accepted as "the father of modern Biblical criticism."

INNOCENT XII AND FRANÇOIS FÉNELON (1651-1715)

Against the rise of active, inquisitive rationalism a Spanish priest named Miguel de Molinos in the 1670s introduced a passive, unquestioning mysticism which soon came to be called quietism because of its glorification of spiritual inertness, making of the human soul an empty receptacle to be filled with the love of God. This idea was hardly unknown in traditional Christian mysticism; Molinos carried it to such extremes, however, as his assertion that a person in a transport of passivity could commit sin without guilt, since the responsibility would have to be assigned to some active agent such as God or the devil. This at least was the charge against him, but in his first hearing before the Holy Office he defended his views so ably that even that unfriendly court acquitted him. In 1687, however, Pope Innocent XI, under pressure from activist Jesuits and from Louis XIV, who took a dim view of the independent individualism implied, condemned Molinos' teachings, and the unfortunate priest spent the remaining ten years of his life in prison.

Since ideas are not so easily imprisoned, Quietism spread quickly among both Catholics and Protestants (especially the Quakers). In France it was taken up by Jeanne Marie Guyon, a wealthy, personable and tirelessly articulate widow whose prolific pen produced a steady flow of what might be called quietistic (not fully quietist) literature. Intellectual discipline was not its outstanding feature: as she put it, she wrote "with unbelievable swiftness" and "a strange impetuosity," creating material that was often incomplete and disconnected because it "flowed from my central depth without passing through my head." Her ideas, representing as they did a fervent though moderate form of quietism, attracted a large following, and many people considered her a living saint. Among them was the Abbé François Fénelon, who lived at the Versailles court as tutor and spiritual counselor to the King's eldest grandson. He was already well acquainted with her reputation and writing when they met at the court in the late 1680s.

A man of mystical bent but high intelligence, Fénelon found most of her writing tediously verbose and unreadable yet considered her basic notions of inner calm and self-denying love very compelling and very Christian, especially in contrast with the harshly militant, oppressive Catholicism all about him. (His Most Catholic Majesty, for instance, had recently revoked that symbol of tolerance, the Edict of Nantes, and Protestants were once again being feverishly persecuted.) An important proponent of militant oppressiveness, as we have already seen, was the formidable bishop Bossuet, whose reaction to Mme. Guyon's impractical, visionary, highly personal, unregimented and noninstitutional form of religion was chiefly rising indignation.

Fénelon and Guyon became firm friends. He helped her increase her influence at Versailles, especially with his friend Mme. de Maintenon, the king's second wife. But he was a good friend also, and indeed a protégé, of the older Bossuet, who now considered him a dupe of the insidious Guyon. This filial friendship must have blinded him to Bossuet's blindness, to the older man's inability to see a glint of Guyon's light under her bushel of obscurities. When the chorus of objections to her writing approached the deafening, Fénelon confidently advised her to submit all her work to Bossuet for evaluation, to what must have been his everlasting, intense regret. Bossuet, a very busy man, spent six grueling, conscientious months struggling through her voluminous literature. The net result was condemnation and submission. This was the beginning of her downfall, which eventually included five years in the Bastille and a final fourteen years thereafter in ill health and relative isolation.

Pope Innocent XII knew of Fénelon, and what he knew he admired. Most of his nine-year reign (1691-1700) was spent staving off Gallicanism, the persistent effort of the French Catholic hierarchy to weaken papal influence in their country. Bossuet was a leader in this effort, supporting the independence of the French monarchy through the divine right of kings, all clearly explained in a tract presumptuously entitled *Politics Drawn from the Words of Holy Scripture*. Although Fénelon was an ultramontane, a supporter of universal papal authority, and might therefore have expected at least some fence-sitting from Innocent, it just so happened that Rome and Versailles had recently negotiated an uneasy truce; the papal coterie therefore advised His Holiness to cooperate with His Most Catholic Majesty as much as possible. Cooperation proved possible when Louis urged condemnation of Fénelon's own writing. In 1699 it was condemned as leaning toward Quietism. Fénelon, by now archbishop of Cambrai, submitted gracefully, devoting himself to his pastoral duties, quietly, until his death in 1715.

Some 250 years later the celebrated mystic Thomas Merton pointed out that the thrust of the writing was quite orthodox, that Rome has "repeatedly taught the doctrine itself as it has been lived and taught by the saints. The most recent of these is Thérèse of Lisieux, whose 'little way' is not only very close to Fénelon, but often echoes him practically word for word. There is no more quietism in Fénelon than there is in the 'little way' or, for that matter, in St. John of the Cross."

(In discussions of cases like this, authority enthusiasts often argue that the censures did not involve papal statements claimed to be infallible, nor any papal judgments of heresy. This is true, and quite irrelevant in this context. Today's papal pronouncements on birth control, abortion, divorce, etc., are not claimed to be infallible, nor have maverick positions on these issues been condemned by a pope as heresy. Those positions are merely indisputably condemned as indisputably erroneous.)

GREGORY XVI AND
FELICITÉ DE LAMENNAIS (1782-1854)

The 18th was not the papacy's happiest century. It was a time of feverish reaction against the traditional church-state tyranny over mind and body. Not only were people insisting on doing some thinking for themselves, they were even demanding some measure of control over the governing of their lives. Europe's monarchs resisted, including the monarchs of the Papal States. In 1773 Pope Clement XIV, yielding to urgent counsel from the corrupt and avaricious Bourbon princes, actually disbanded the Jesuits, his most faithful supporters, in what later popes have described as one of Catholicism's sorriest episodes of papal subservience to the divinely rightful establishment. The century's revolutions, culminating in the excesses of the French Revolution, had no more use for popes than for other kings, the contempt generally trickling down through the ranks to bishops and priests.

After Napoleon finally restored some order and decreed some tolerance for the Church by the end of the century, even he managed to make his coronation a scene of acute humiliation for the papacy.

The Congress of Vienna in 1815 put most of the monarchs back in place, and Rome felt comfortable again. But some Catholic thinkers, seeing this as only a temporary respite, argued that Rome should begin accommodating itself to the liberal ideas bubbling just below the surface and thus be prepared to live with the new order when the thrones began to topple. Prominent among these liberal thinkers was a French priest and writer named Felicité de Lamennais. Through the 1820s he argued ever more urgently for Church recognition, or at least tolerance, of such liberal ideas as the separation of church and state; freedom of religion, speech, thought, education, association, and of course the press; and democracy based on universal suffrage. In 1831 he and some of his disciples started a daily paper, *The Future (L'Avenir)*, under a masthead of "God and Freedom." "Let us not tremble before liberalism," he exhorted the readers of his editorials, "let us Catholicize it."

The French hierarchy would countenance neither activity. Stiff resistance, that was their ticket, and to the stake with compromisers. (Well, *that* had gone out of style, but whatever was practicable.) Separation of church and state indeed—who would pay their clergy's salaries if not the state? Selling *The Future* was banned on all church property, and its future looked dim. Lamennais, a vocal supporter of papal supremacy against Gallican notions of supreme councils composed of national hierarchies, was inspired to appeal to Rome. What he did not realize, or had neglected to remember, was that Gregory XVI opposed all liberal thinking, which he associated with church-burning revolution, and was at that moment cooperating with Austria's royal military forces in suppressing a revolt in the Papal States. Like most authorities, he was against violence, but the highly visible violence of rebellion more than the insidious violence of oppression.

After arriving in Rome, Lamennais and two of his friends in early 1832 wrote a long appeal to the pope to make a formal pronouncement in favor of the separation of church and state. The overthrow of the Bourbon monarchy in the revolution of July 1830, they argued, made such a pronouncement more impera-tive than ever if the Church was to survive in the world of the future.

Gregory was not about to get on any such bandwagon. He found time to reply late that summer in an encyclical, *Mirari Vos,* denouncing liberal Catholicism with shrill intemperance, branding it as perverse, "unbridled license" which invited "the most frightful immorality" and menaced legitimate princely authority with "an ever-approaching revolution-abyss of bottom-less miseries . . . in which heresy and sects have so to speak vomited as into a sewer all that their bosom holds of license, sacrilege and blasphemy." It need hardly be added that His Nauseated Holiness vehemently condemned any separation of church and state, reviling freedom of conscience as insanity and freedom of the press as an abomination. Any disagreement with these pontifications was flatly forbidden.

Lamennais returned to Paris, where he stopped publication of *The Future.* Although submitting formally to the papal demand, he could not stop all thought processes. After long meditation he decided that he must speak and write not as a Roman Catholic but as a French citizen criticizing the social and political iniquities of the times, thus escaping the rigors of papal jurisdiction. He discovered, however, that there was no such escape, for he was still a priest. His activities attracted Rome's untiring olfactory attention, his bishop received a letter from His Complaining Holiness, and he was suspended from his priestly functions until he again submitted to the pope. Quite beaten down, he did so.

But he had written a tract against the harm done to the working poor by competitive capitalism, calling on laborers to demand their rights, and it was published in the spring of 1834. It soon became a best-seller, and within a couple of months His Reignited Holiness issued another vituperative encyclical *(Singulari Nos)*, this one particularly condemning the tract as "small in size but immense in perversity" and as promoting notions that were "false, calumnious, rash, inducing to anarchy, contrary to the Word of God, impious, scandalous, and erroneous." The proper activity of Catholics was simply stated and could be simply carried out: "submission to authority."

This was not a fatal blow to liberal Catholicism, but it seems to have left Lamennais in a state of lethargic despair. He was never formally excommunicated but rather drifted away from the rigidities of creed and ritual. He did manage to survive another twenty years.

It would be another century before the Second Vatican Council would declare that "the political community and the Church are mutually independent and self-governing"; that "all the faithful, clerical and lay, possess a lawful freedom of inquiry and thought, and the freedom to express their minds humbly and courageously about those matters in which they enjoy competence"; and that "civil authority is duty bound to defend and protect a true and just availability of information . . . especially as regards freedom of the press." The spinning noise was Gregory in his grave.

PIUS IX AND ANTONIO ROSMINI-SERBATI (1797-1855)

The contrast between Gregory and the man who succeeded him in 1846 was striking and, for all but the stoniest authoritarians, heartening. Gregory was unsociable, even reclusive, as one might presume after reading his paranoid pronouncements; Pius was personable, even genial, a politician who enjoyed mingling with his people in the streets of Rome, at least during his first two years.

Among his admirers was a priest from northern Italy named Antonio Rosmini-Serbati, who managed to combine liberal thinking, fervent enthusiasm for the unification of Italy, and servile devotion to the papal establishment into a single ideological potpourri. In 1828 he founded the Rosminians, more formally known as the Institute of Charity, a religious order dedicated to educational and charitable work and bound by vows of poverty, chastity, and obedience to ecclesiastical superiors. The Rosminians resembled the Jesuits closely enough to arouse some resentment among some powerful Jesuits in Rome who were not disposed to welcome an upstart rival. Moreover, Rosmini was a voluminous writer—some 50,000 pages in his lifetime—and his writing brought him not only a reputation but also favorable attention from three successive popes, thereby causing a measure of consternation among Their Eminences in the curia. Pius IX was especially attracted to his ideas during those first two years, to the point of offering him a red hat, an offer which Their Eminences were even more anxious than Rosmini to have withdrawn. But during the papal exile at Gaeta, a coastal town south of Rome, his enemies at court managed to turn His Disillusioned Holiness against him.

Two of his books, published in early 1848, were relegated to the Index the following year. One was *A Constitution for Social Justice,* in which he argued for the unification of Italy under a parliamentary government subject to the authority of the pope. The Holy Office liked the part about papal authority but not the part about a republican government or, for that matter, the idea of a unified Italy. The other book was *The Five Wounds of the Church,* in which he criticized the segregation of clergy and laity in ritual, the deficiences in the education of the clergy, the disharmony existing among bishops, princely influence in the appointment of bishops, and ecclesiastical preoccupation with wealth. These criticisms, although hardly extraordinary, were enough to heighten Eminent bloodpressures, including that of the pope's good rightist arm, Cardinal Giacomo Antonelli.

His Ambivalent Holiness played a very ambiguous role in all this, granting Rosmini friendly audiences, warning him of "the things they say about you," asking him to issue corrections without specifying corrections of what, and in the end approving the proscription of his books. Rosmini repaid the pope's vacillating disloyalty with utter loyalty, submitting to the decree totally and even offering to publish any retraction specified by the Holy

Office (none ever was so specified). He soon departed the papal court, never to return.

That court was returned to power in Rome by French armed forces in the spring of 1850. Although it was preoccupied with resuming its role of political authority, parts of it still seethed with anti-Rosmini invective: he was called a stubborn ignoramus, a spreader of infernal teachings, Jansenist wolf, a hypocritical imposter, a traitor to the Church, and other less than friendly things. The pope bore up under the hullaballoo until March 1851, when he issued a ukase ordering everyone to shut up and announcing that a formal examination of Rosmini's works would be undertaken. This time his genuine affection for Rosmini, who by all accounts was a very gentle, personable and saintly man, seems to have taken over, for he apparently was confident that the examinee would be vindicated, having expressed some private regret over the proscribing of the two books in 1849. The procedure took more than three years, while pro-Rosminians tried to get it over with and the anti-Rosminians contributed monkey-wrenches. Examiners died and were replaced, but finally, in July 1854, Pius was able to issue a decree completely vindicating his irregularly supported friend and reversing all the reasons for proscribing any of his works. "Rosmini," he remarked to a fellow bishop, "is not only a good Catholic, but a saint. God uses saints to assure the triumph of truth." The harassed saint died the following year.

The saint's enemies, however, would not give up. After what they considered a decent interval, they resumed their attacks until, in the 1870s, Pius told them to stop already. But in 1888, with Leo XIII's approval, they managed to get forty propositions extracted from his works condemned formally by the Holy See. Among the heinous positions he was accused of holding were favoring the use of vernaculars in the liturgy and the separation of church and state. He had earlier denied such charges, although he would hardly have to do so today.

PIUS X AND ALFRED LOISY (1857-1940)

To this day there are fundamentalists who stoutly hold that the earth *is too* flat, because the Bible speaks of its four corners. A hundred years ago or so such opinions were not automatically a sign of intellectual dishevelment; among Catholics they represented the prevalent and officially encouraged view, despite burgeoning evidence to the contrary. Once again deductive hallucination was pitted against inductive observation and reflection.

Among the victims of militant ignorance was a French priest named Alfred Loisy, who like many others was in the awkward position of being a Catholic biblical scholar at a time when Rome and most other Church authorities considered Biblical scholarship to be the work of the devil. Yet he, as well as others, was knowledgeable enough and intelligent enough to be prescient enough to worry that a Catholicism irrevocably wedded to a literal interpretation of the Bible, based on centuries-old theological musings, could be headed for the institutional scrapheap. Although he admired the celebrated Ernest Renan's scholarship, for instance, he deplored the older man's agnosticism, arguing that the one need not result in the other. Like Cardinal Newman, whom he also admired, he saw a Bible full of peripheral data (Newman's "obiter dicta") unrelated to its essential function of communicating

God's will to humanity, and to these passages, many of them patently unreliable, "inspiration" hardly needed to be ascribed, at least in the sense of purveying truth.

Like Newman, too, he saw a changing tradition, an historical development of Christian doctrine that belied the conception of a final, complete, absolute theology received directly from the Apostles and subject only to interpretive refinements. Authoritative theology, he submitted, must not be blind to signs of the times but must be sensitive to the implications of scientific and other secular discoveries. Truth and doctrine are not one and the same; truth is unchanging, but a doctrine, as an expression of truth, is subject to the exigencies of its time and place. The authority of the Church, he insisted, lies precisely in its ability to express the truth in terms appropriate to time and place. The ideal is not perpetual conformity but rather living unity.

Similarly the Gospels, conditioned by their time and place, must be read and interpreted in the light of historical circumstances. At least it is comforting, in contemplating the advice to pluck out one's offending eye, to know that hyperbole was fashionable in the writing of the age; such activities as plucking are not required, Origen's famous self-emasculation to the contrary notwithstanding. (It may be worth noting again that, for all the insistence that Scripture is inspired, the concept of inspiration has never been defined; it seems to range from direct dictation to general impulse.)

The turn of the century saw the publication of some now famous lectures by the Protestant theologian Adolf von Harnack, whose Biblical studies had led him to conclude that the institutional church was without foundation, its claims resting on "a case not of distortion but of total perversion." Late in 1902 Loisy's answer was published, defending the Catholic Church as an institution arising necessarily out of the gospel community, a defense based on historical research. It did not, however, and indeed could not defend the rigid, intransigent institution beloved by the archconservatives. As might be expected, this failure got him into trouble. As late as the 1950s a true-blue Catholic historian accused him of having merely pretended to defend Catholicism in order to promote Harnack's nefarious ideas.

Late in 1903 five of his works were consigned to the Index, including the defense against Harnack. No explanation was offered, in line with another endearing tradition. Loisy replied with a formal submission but, unlike Rosmini, made it as clear as he could that the submission was disciplinary, that scholarship and conscience would not permit an "internal assent." Although he continued to say Mass, he doubtless was losing whatever vestigial enthusiasm he may have felt for ecclesiastical authority and doctrinal paraphernalia.

Meanwhile the anti-Loisy, anti-Modernist cabal in Rome prepared a list of 65 Infernal Errors for Pius X's signature. Issued in July 1907, it strewed its condemnations about with little discrimination, in some cases proscribing opinions which no one seems ever to have held. ("Modernism" was Rome's catch-all term for contemporary enemies, like "Communism" a generation later.) Although most of the list is largely meaningless today, it does contain a number of interesting assertions behind its negative interdictions. For example:

Rome's Biblical interpretations may not be modified by Biblical research (#2).

The conclusions of secular science are subject to Rome's authority (#5).

Rome can rightfully demand "internal assent from the faithful" (#7).

Divine inspiration guarantees that the Bible is "free from every error" (#11).

Rome's revealed dogmas are "truths which have fallen from heaven" (#22).

Rome is the head of all churches by divine law (#56).

The following September His Holiness handed down an accessory encyclical written in an abusive style almost worthy of his predecessor Gregory XVI. What worried him, he wrote in the customary paranoid vein, was not only the "notable increase in the number of enemies of the Cross of Christ who, by arts entirely new and full of deceit, are striving to destroy the vital energy of the Church," but also the "many who belong to the Catholic laity and, what is more sad, to the ranks of the priesthood itself, who, animated by a false zeal for the Church and lacking the solid safeguards of philosophy and theology—nay, more, thoroughly imbued with the poisonous doctrines taught by the enemies of the Church and lost to all sense of modesty—put themselves forward as reformers of the Church."

Foremost among such poison-laden miscreants was Alfred Loisy, who was formally excommunicated in March 1908. In the heyday of the Inquisition he surely would have been fed to the flames. But church and state were separate now in France and elsewhere, and shortly after his excommunication he was appointed to the chair of the History of Religions at the College of France, from which he retired some twenty years later to a small property on the Marne. He died in June 1940, in distress over Germany's third invasion of France in his lifetime.

PIUS XI AND PIERRE
TEILHARD DE CHARDIN (1881-1955)

The 1920s were a period of transition for Roman hardshells, as the bugbear of Modernism slowly was forced to share hostility honors with the bugbear of Communism. Among the issues keeping the former alive was evolution. On this one Rome had plenty of support from out of the darker recesses of deductive catatonia. Tennessee's notorious Scopes trial was held in 1925, and that state's law banning the teaching of evolution remained in force until 1967.

The sticky problem of reconciling the Genesis account of universal creation with the evidence rapidly being accumulated by scientific research (not always totally objective but always intellectually accountable) bothered many Christian archeologists and paleontologists. Many of the Catholics among them were especially troubled, anxiously anticipating a confrontation with Rome's Our-Mind's-Made-Up intransigence. Into this uneasy environment came a French Jesuit priest-paleontologist named Pierre Teilhard de Chardin.

Teilhard himself was an uneasy mixture of hard-headed scientist and mystical poet. His scientific studies, especially during an 18-month visit to China in 1923-24, convinced him beyond reasonable doubt of the general validity of the evolutionary theory, a conviction requiring some accommodation with his faith in Scripture and his role as preacher and teacher—and as writer, for he was tireless scribbler. Eventually he would produce the philosophical construction for which he became famous. It would be a visionary, mystical, less-than-crystal-clear amalgam of science and religion, proposing the human spirit as the pinnacle of evolutionary development, glorified in the risen Christ. His theory was never formally and absolutely condemned because Rome could never get a handle on it. The most the Holy Office did about it was to issue an inspired banality, seven years after his death, to the effect that his works should not be read uncritically.

In 1924 he experienced some preliminary trouble with the tattler network. Late that year he returned from China to Paris to complete his university studies and to write countless unpublished essays urging a reconciliation of science and religion, and deploring Rome's inflexibility. (Because of Roman restrictions, all his major work remained unpublished during his lifetime.) Since the accession of Pius XI in 1922, that inflexibility had been hardening like newly poured cement. Late in 1923 a biblical handbook by a respected scholar, after being used for some ten years in seminaries, was relegated to the Index for tolerating flexibility in interpreting Scripture. In the summer of 1924 a papal letter warned scriptural scholars against thinking they knew anything, citing St. Paul's disparaging remarks on the subject (I Cor 8:1, 2) and backing a Holy Office decree issued earlier that deplored the "dangerous" questioning which threatened the Catholic faith. Beyond this, in the political arena, Pius and his Vatican Jesuits were preparing for the bedfellow arrangement with Italian fascism that would produce the long-sought restoration of papal political sovereignty.

In November 1924 Teilhard received a summons to Lyon from his provincial, his immediate Jesuit superior. Two years earlier he had been asked by a couple of fellow Jesuits to record his thoughts on original sin. Among possible interpretations of that doctrine as it relates to Genesis, he suggested that the Biblical account of the fall of Adam and Eve could be a symbolic explanation of human immorality and the existence of pain and death. In other words, not necessarily literally true. Most mysteriously, a copy of this informal, tentative paper (the full contents of which have yet to be divulged) had wound up in Rome, and now he was being called on the carpet for such wild talk.

In Lyon, his provincial's summons instructed him, he would be expected to promise in writing never again to write or even say a word out of line with Rome's standard interpretation. After some agonizing, he offered a substitute statement that his paper merely argued for the possibility of harmonizing doctrine and data—adding a promise to limit any discussion of such conjecture to professional meetings. The provincial read this cheeky substitute and, after lowering his eyebrows, agreed to forward it to Rome. Teilhard returned to Paris, to do some dangerous thinking.

And some writing. And some conducting of seminars. And, unintentionally but inevitably, some attracting of attention and some garnering of a reputation, for he was a stimulating, popular teacher. The reputation reached tender episcopal ears, and a corps of alarmed French conservative bishops in turn alarmed the Holy Office, which in its turn alarmed the Vatican Jesuits. The Jesuit General, top pooh-bah of the Society of Jesus and an ideological buddy of the pope's, wrote Teilhard a letter explaining how the "deposit of faith" could save a faithful Catholic a lot of "useless" thinking. He also wrote the provincial, instructing him to demand Teilhard's submission to Rome's requirement for a declaration of faith in (as one biographer put it) "the literal truth of the Book of Genesis—Adam, Eve, forbidden fruit, and all." Furthermore, Teilhard was to cease his work in Paris and get out of the country.

And so Teilhard got out of the country. He would be in China for the next twenty years. In 1950 Pius XII declared in an encyclical that evolution, at the physical level, had become an "open question," and in the 1960s Vatican II declared, in connection with Biblical interpretation, that "truth is proposed and expressed in a variety of ways." For example, symbolically.

PIUS XII AND JOHN COURTNEY MURRAY (1904-67)

The American constitutional prohibition against a state establishment of religion was never a source of unalloyed joy in Rome, where the prevailing judgment was that "error has no rights," error essentially being any opinion but Rome's. The still-rather-new United States harbored a very non-Roman opinion on the compatibility of religion and democracy, enhanced by the separation of church and state. Rome's experience with democracy in Europe had been largely with the kind of radical democracy that dispossesses bishops and empties churches, as in the French Revolution. Its attitude therefore was that Roman Catholicism should be the state religion, really the only religion, wherever Catholics made up the majority; where Catholics were in the minority, Rome wanted a Catholic monarch able to do his Catholic duty but otherwise would tolerate an uncomfortable pluralism until the evil could be remedied.

In the late 1800s probably most American Catholic church-men shared this attitude, but quite a few held that Catholicism could and should compete freely (and peacefully) with other religions in a religiously neutral political society—even in America, where the neutrality rested in basic law rather than in practical politics. When a biography of Isaac Hecker—a prominent American liberal clergyman of the time, the founder of the Paulist Fathers, and a great believer in America's pluralistic separation of church and state—reached Europe in a French translation, it became quite a best-seller among Catholic liberals. This so alarmed French bishops, by and large a recalcitrant lot of wistful monarchists, that they cranked up their tattling service in Rome, eventually persuading Pope Leo XIII in 1899 to issue a con-demnation of "Americanism." This was Rome's term for a collection of opinions which were mostly figments of its siege mentality, inspired more by heated accusations than by beliefs held by American Catholics. The condemnation set the stage for the next couple of generations, which saw an increasing effort on the part of some American Catholics to persuade Rome that the Church could and should live with, and indeed encourage, democracy. The growth in the Catholic ability to cope with pluralism can be seen in the contrast between the 1928 defeat of Al Smith and the 1960 election of Jack Kennedy for the U.S. Presidency. One of the people consulted by the Kennedy camp in preparing his famous Houston speech to a meeting of Protestant ministers was the prominent Jesuit theologian, Rev.

John Courtney Murray, who had just published an air-clearing book, *We Hold These Truths: Catholic Reflections on the American Proposition.*

Murray was an outspoken advocate of church-state separation, especially in a long-running journalistic debate with his principal adversary on the subject, Rev. Joseph Fenton, editor of *The American Ecclesiastical Review.* Fenton's position, firmly embedded in Roman Catholic tradition, was essentially the Roman viewpoint described above, a viewpoint shared especially by the state-supported bishops of Franco Spain. Murray countered that church-state separation (in America if not in Spain), far from being an unmitigated evil to be tolerated only when inescapable, should be welcomed by Roman Catholicism as an opportunity to avoid the corrupting temptations and stresses of political power and to focus on the spiritual teaching mission assigned by Jesus Christ. This implied an imperative need for Catholic (Roman) approval of religious freedom, of the right of a person to hold his or her religious beliefs without coercion. It also implied that the Church (Rome) would have to accept an important development, a basic change in an all-but-infallibly declared doctrine.

It may have been this last bit of effrontery that got Rome's dander up, added to the menacing idea of religious tolerance. In March 1953 Alfredo Ottaviani, then one of Rome's fastest-rising cardinal mossbacks and later Joseph Ratzinger's predecessor as No. 2 doctrinal honcho, gave a speech promoting the Spanish ideal of state-supported Catholicism and all but citing Murray personally as a sower of error (which, as we have seen, has no rights). The next month Murray was hospitalized as a result of "extreme fatigue, rooted in a cardiac insufficiency," and was ordered to take a rest, which lasted four months.

At about that time, although he had written nothing but personal letters during his illness and recovery, he began receiving letters from the Rome office of the Jesuit General (the order, founded by an ex-soldier, sports a military ambience). The letters at first contained gentle warnings and hints of pressure on the General, who in any case was likely to find Murray's church-state views distasteful. In November came an order to explain his position fully in a letter to the General. In reply Murray, busily trying to meet a deadline for an article on Leo XIII, asked for time to prepare a careful exposition of his viewpoint. Because the order was ambiguous, involving not only Murray but also the magazine *America,* a Jesuit journal, and Ambassador Clare Booth Luce, he also asked uncertainly if he was really suspected of heresy. (*America's* editor had impertinently taken a Spanish cardinal to task for declaring, in a Lenten pastoral, that only Catholics had a right to religious freedom; Ambassador Luce had apparently exhibited some Christian tolerance toward some Pentecostals in Rome.) The response to his anxious inquiry was reassuring: no, no, heresy's not involved, you have nothing to worry about.

Meanwhile Pope Pius XII, whose compulsion to indoctrinate was displayed in an overwhelming flood of longwinded encyclicals, had been issuing statements on church and state ambiguous enough for both Fenton and Murray to claim support. In his not-so-public dealings, however, he may have been less ambiguous. In April 1954, soon after Murray had delivered a lecture at Catholic University supporting a liberal interpretation of the papal remarks, Cardinal Spellman of New York received a complaint against Murray from Ottaviani; in reply the old pro Spellman requested a clarification, which apparently was never given. In Rome the pressure on the General rose, but the mills of the Roman gods, as usual, ground slowly. In the summer of 1955, shortly after receiving an honorary LL.D. from St. Louis University for attaining "to the very first rank of American theologians and religious spokesmen," Murray was ordered by Rome to shut his mouth on the subject of church and state and, insofar as it was involved, on religious freedom. He was free to exercise his talents in whatever other way he wished. "I suppose," he was told by an aide to the General, presumably with tongue in cheek, "you may write poetry."

Being a good soldier, he complied with the order, although he continued writing and speaking on other subjects over the next three years—at the end of which, in October 1958, Pius XII was succeeded by John XXIII, who, the following January, announced the convening of Vatican II.

Murray was initially invited to the Council's first session and then, embarrassingly but firmly, disinvited, for he was still in the curial doghouse. But then some cardinal American efforts (chiefly Spellman's) got him invited as an expert consultant to the remaining three sessions, and he became the generally acknowledged "author" of the Council's Declaration on Religious Freedom. Like most committee statements, it was wordy, but it managed a comparatively concise assertion of its general principle: "This Vatican Synod declares that the human person has a right to religious freedom. This freedom means that all men [and women, even for Rome] are to be immune from coercion on the part of individuals or of social groups and of any human power, in such wise that in religious matters no one is to be forced to act in a manner contrary to his own beliefs." Amen.

Afterword

Mass on Sunday, fish on Friday, fasting throughout Lent, all were ancient Catholic traditions until a generation ago. Today Lent has only two fastdays, only 13% of the year's Fridays are meatless, and a devout Catholic is free to attend Mass on Saturday evening and forget about Sunday. So much for Catholic tradition.

Yet it is precisely unwavering Catholic tradition that Rome cites as its rock of ages, as the source of its unwavering authority. It used to be fashionable among Catholic apologists to stress the distinction between the absolute authority of infallibly proclaimed doctrines (very rare) and the less demanding authority of everything else (very common). Rome has more recently recognized this distinction, however, as an invitation to unregulated thinking and has increasingly insisted on absolute acceptance ("internal assent") of just about anything it has to say. This might work well in an institution for the religiously unhinged, but in the real world it has brought on what is usually called a crisis of authority. Again.

It is hardly surprising that Charles Curran holds on desperately to the distinction of noninfallible teaching or that Hans Küng proposes an imperfect but generally reliable "indefectibility"—or that both would maintain that although the *Church* may be ultimately infallible, the Church and Rome are two quite different things. It was not Rome against which Jesus promised that the gates of hell would not prevail. The total certainty that Rome cherishes in itself and requires in others is an affair of the heart, and, Barry Goldwater fans to the contrary notwithstanding ("In Your Heart You Know He's Right"), the heart is a notoriously unreliable source of credible information. Rome's heartfelt leadership gave the world Christendom but has yet to give it Christianity. As a noted defender of Catholicism, G. K. Chesterton, once wrote, Christianity has not failed, it has simply never been tried. At least on an institutional scale.

It might have been tried if Rome had been more dedicated to the promotion of Christ's message of divine and human love than to its own concerns over crowns, coffers, cornerstones, costumes, claims, comforts, comestibles, concubines, cousins, commands, catechisms, cardinals and crusades. Yet the message might have been lost altogether if Rome had not been there to provide some continuity, some spiritual focus through centuries of fantastic beliefs and brutal behavior. Great popes, good popes, mediocre popes and even some bad popes have contributed to this basic function. With all its faults, Rome is several cuts above, say, the old leadership of the Soviet Union, the present leadership of Iran, or the recently deposed leadership of various evangelical enterprises.

If it had not become so jealous of its power, property, perks and prerogatives, and of its claims to divine guidance, it might have done less harm to the Church, as in its urgent invitation to the Reformation. If today it were less preoccupied with asserting its authority and more concerned with relating Christ's message of love to the moral problems of our time—consumerism, promiscuity, racism, sexism, family irresponsibility, self-centeredness, etc.—it might glimpse that message in the opinions that it so eagerly condemns. It might *learn* something. Inductively.

It might learn, for instance, to think in terms of individuals, to recognize that circumstances can alter cases without raising the specter of situation ethics. People vary enormously in capabilities, vulnerabilities, sensibilities, and adaptabilities, and the situations in which they find themselves vary even more. Rome's flat assertion that the "ensoulment" of a human occurs at conception, for instance, thus equating all induced abortion with murder, allows for no practical distinction between the mother of a large family whose pregnancy seriously threatens her life and the childless woman who merely wants her first child to be a boy, to please her husband. It makes no provision for the medical evidence that pregnancies, probably more often than not, end in natural abortion, especially in cases of mental or physical defectives, evidence suggesting that induced abortions can often assist nature, not frustrate it. Given the Catholic traditions that what distinguishes the human from other animals is reason and that a person does not reach "the age of reason" until the age of seven, how can Rome hold so rigidly to the "ensoulment at conception" proposition?

It might learn that some young people can make irrevocable commitments to celibacy or monogamy more reliably than others, and that really the only way to discover a person's capacity in this respect is by trial and error; this may lead to some irresponsible behavior, but surely *that* is where some guidance is genuinely needed. It might decide that "putting asunder" means "forcing apart," that first marriages can be disasters and remarriages great successes (consider Ron and Nancy), and that professional celibacy is not the optimum vantage point for issuing unilateral ukases on married life. It might turn down the volume on its inner voices long enough to be aware of the commotion outside. For the commotion outside—Curran, Küng, Schillebeeckx, et al.— has a lot to offer. Compassionate intelligence, for instance, exercised in an effort to adapt to the human condition without utterly succumbing to it.

But Rome has a lot to offer, too. Without Rome's miraculous survivability, Catholicism surely would have deteriorated into a miscellany of quarreling sects without even a debatable claim to any authority. Rome does provide a refuge for the countless millions who are unable or unwilling to think for themselves, to take on the burdens of personal responsibility. It gives most Catholics a sense of belonging to a Judeo-Christian tradition which, uniquely, stretches back for thousands of years. It has provided sacraments to heal the soul and prepare it for its destiny. Like the leaven to which Christ compared his kingdom, the Church under Rome's leadership has sustained Christianity for the spiritual nourishment of mankind. That leadership generally has been of the kind that has trouble keeping up with its followers, but braking can be as useful a function of leadership as accelerating.

It can be and is argued that with Rome's heavy foot so rigidly on the brake the Church will never get anywhere, and that is just what John Paul & Co. seem to have in mind. Yet Rome's intransigence in the past has not prevented Catholicism from eventually coming to terms with such terrors as interest on loans, church-state separation, democracy and freedom of religion. Since so many of yesterday's mavericks have ultimately been vindicated, there is at least hope for many of today's.

Bibliography

Aradi, Zsolt. *Pius XI, the Pope and the Man*. Garden City, N.Y.: Hanover House, 1958.

Aretin, Karl von. *The Papacy and the Modern World*. New York: McGraw-Hill Book Co., 1970.

Attwater, Donald. *A Dictionary of the Popes*. London: The Catholic Book Club, 1939.

Baker, Derek (ed.). *Schism, Heresy and Religious Protest: Papers Read at the Tenth Summer and the Eleventh Winter Meetings of the Ecclesiastical Historical Society*. Cambridge University Press, 1972.

Barmann, Lawrence F. *Baron Friedrich Von Hügel and the Modernist Crisis in England*. Cambridge University Press, 1972.

Barrett, William E. *Shepherd of Mankind: A Biography of Pope Paul VI*. Garden City, N.Y.: Doubleday & Co., 1964.

Boff, Leonardo. *Church: Charism and Power, Liberation Theology and the Institutional Church*. New York: Crossroads Publishing Co., 1985.

————. *Jesus Christ Liberator: A Critical Christology for Our Time*. Maryknoll, N.Y.: Orbis Books, 1978.

Boff, Leonardo. *Liberating Grace.* Maryknoll, N.Y.: Orbis Books, 1979.

Boff, Leonardo and Clodovis Boff. *Salvation and Liberation.* Maryknoll, N.Y.: Orbis Book, 1984.

Bokenkotter, Thomas. *A Concise History of the Catholic Church.* Garden City, N.Y.: Doubleday & Co., 1977.

Bonpane, Blase. *Guerillas of Peace: Liberation Theology and the Central American Revolution.* Boston: South End Press, 1985.

Braybrook, Neville. *Teilhard de Chardin: Pilgrim of the Future.* New York: Seabury Press, 1964.

Broderick, James. *Galileo: The Man, His Work, His Misfortunes.* London: The Catholic Book Club, 1964.

Brown, Harold J. *Heresies: The Image of Christ in the Mirror of Heresy and Orthodoxy from the Apostles to the Present.* Garden City, N.Y.: Doubleday & Co., 1984.

Brown, Robert McAfee. "Father Charles Curran and Canon 812." *The Christian Century,* Feb. 4-11, 1987.

———. *Gustavo Gutiérrez.* Atlanta: John Knox Press, 1980.

Brusher, Joseph S. *Popes Through the Ages.* New York: D. Van Nostrand Co., 1959.

Bury, John B. *History of the Papacy in the 19th Century.* New York: Schocken Books, 1964.

Burton, Katherine. *Great Mantle: Pope Pius X.* New York: Longman, Inc., 1950.

———. *Witness of the Light: The Life of Pope Pius XII.* New York: Longman, Green & Co., 1958.

Carmody, John. *Contemporary Catholic Theology.* San Francisco: Harper & Row, 1980.

Chamberlin, E. R. *The Bad Popes.* New York: Dial Press, 1969.

Cheetham, Nicholas. *Keepers of the Keys: A History of the Popes from St. Peter to John Paul II.* New York: Charles Scribner's Sons, 1982.

Christiani, Leon. *Pierre Teilhard, His Life and Spirit.* New York: Macmillan Co., 1960.

Christie-Murray, David. *A History of Heresy.* London: New English Library, 1976.

Coppa, Frank J. *Pope Pius IX, Crusader in a Secular Age.* Boston: Twayne Publishers, 1979.

Cox, Harvey. *Religion in the Secular City: Toward a Postmodern Theology.* New York: Simon & Schuster, 1984.

Craig, Mary. *Man from a Far Country: An Informal Portrait of Pope John Paul II.* New York: William Morrow & Co., 1979.

Cuenot, Claude. *Teilhard de Chardin, a Biographical Study.* Baltimore: Helicon Press, 1965.

Curran, Charles E. (ed.). *Absolutes in Moral Theology?* Washington, D.C.: Corpus Books, 1968.

———. *Contemporary Problems in Moral Theology.* Notre Dame, Ind.: Fides Publishers, 1970.

———. (ed.) *Contraception: Authority and Dissent.* New York: Herder & Herder, 1969.

———. *Critical Concerns in Moral Theology.* Notre Dame, Ind.: University of Notre Dame Press, 1984.

———. "Masturbation and Objectively Grave Matter: An Exploratory Discussion." *Proceedings of the Catholic Theological Society of America,* 1966, pp. 95-112.

———. *Moral Theology: A Continuing Journey.* Notre Dame, Ind.: University of Notre Dame Press, 1982.

———. *New Perspectives in Moral Theology.* Notre Dame, Ind.: Fides Publishers, 1974.

———. *Ongoing Revision in Moral Theology.* Notre Dame, Ind.: Fides Publishers, 1975.

Curran, Charles E., Robert E. Hunt, *et al. Dissent in and for the Church.* New York: Sheed & Ward, 1969.

Davidson, Thomas. *The Philosophical System of Antonio Rosmini-Serbati.* London: Kegan Paul, Trench & Co., 1882.

De Cesare, R. *The Last Days of Papal Rome.* New York: Houghton Mifflin Co., 1909.

Doyle, Charles H. *The Life of Pope Pius XII.* New York: Didier Publishing Co., 1945.

Dwyer, John C. *Church History: Twenty Centuries of Catholic Christianity.* New York: Paulist Press, 1985.

Fahey, M. "Richard Simon, Biblical Exegete." *Irish Ecclesiastical Review,* April 1963, pp. 136-147.

Falconi, Carlo. *Popes in the 20th Century.* New York: Little, Brown & Co., 1967.

Fénelon, François. *Letters of Love and Counsel.* New York: Harcourt, Brace & World, 1964.

Fern, Deane W. *Contemporary American Theologies: A Critical Survey.* New York: Seabury Press, 1981. (Chapter 7: "Roman Catholic Theology," pp. 112-134.)

Foy, Felician A. (ed.). *1986 Catholic Almanac.* Huntington, Ind.: Our Sunday Visitor Publishing Co., 1985.

Fremantle, Anne. *The Papal Encyclicals in Their Historical Context.* New York: New American Library, 1963.

Frossard, André. *Be Not Afraid: Pope John Paul II Speaks Out on His Life, His Beliefs, and His Inspiring Vision for Humanity.* New York: St. Martin's Press, 1984.

Giordani, Igino. *Pius X, Country Priest.* Milwaukee: Bruce Publishing Co., 1954.

Gontard, Friedrich. *The Chair of Peter: A History of the Papacy.* New York: Holt, Rinehart & Winston, 1964.

Greeley, Andrew. *The Making of the Popes 1978.* Kansas City: Andrews & McMeel, 1979.

Grenet, Paul B. *Teilhard de Chardin, the Man and His Theories*. New York: V. S. Ericksson, 1966.

Gudorf, Christine E. *Catholic Social Teaching on Liberation Themes*. Washington, D.C.: University Press of America, 1981.

Gutiérrez, Gustavo. *The Power of the Poor in History*. Maryknoll, N.Y.: Orbis Books, 1983.

———. *A Theology of Liberation: History, Politics and Salvation*. Maryknoll, N.Y.: Orbis Books, 1973.

———. *We Drink from Our Own Wells: The Spiritual Journey of a People*. Maryknoll, N.Y.: Orbis Books, 1984.

Haight, Roger. *An Alternate Vision: An Interpretation of Liberation Theology*. New York: Paulist Press, 1985.

Hales, E. E. Y. *The Catholic Church in the Modern World: A Survey from the French Revolution to the Present*. Garden City, N.Y.: Hanover House, 1958.

———. *Pio Nono*. Garden City, N.Y.: Doubleday & Co., 1962.

Halecki, Oscar, and James F. Murray, Jr. *Pius XII: Eugene Pacelli, Pope of Peace*. New York: Farrar, Straus & Young, 1954.

Hatch, Alden. *Pope Paul VI*. New York: Random House, 1966.

Hatch, Alden, and Seamus Walshe. *Crown of Glory: The Life of Pope Pius XII*. New York: Hawthorne Books, 1957.

Hebblethwaite, Peter. *In the Vatican*. Bethseda, Md.: Adler & Adler, 1986.

———. *The New Inquisition?: The Case of Edward Schillebeeckx and Hans Küng*. New York: Harper & Row, 1980.

———. *The Year of the Three Popes*. Cleveland: William Collins, 1979.

Hebblethwaite, Peter, and Ludwig Kaufmann. *John Paul II: A Pictorial Biography*. New York: McGraw-Hill Book Co., 1979.

Hogan, Richard M., and John M. LeVoir. *Covenant of Love: Pope John Paul II on Sexuality, Marriage and Family in the Modern World*. Garden City, N.Y.: Doubleday & Co., 1985.

Holmes, J. Derek. *The Papacy in the Modern World, 1914-78.* New York: Crossword Press, 1981.

Holmes, J. Derek, and Bernard W. Bickers. *A Short History of the Catholic Church.* New York: Paulist Press, 1984.

Holmes, J. Derek. *The Triumph of the Holy See: A Short History of the Papacy in the 19th Century.* Shepherdstown, W.V.: Patmos Press, 1978.

Hughes, Philip E. *A Popular History of the Catholic Church.* New York: Macmillan Publishing Co., 1947.

Hunerman, Wilhelm. *Flame of White: Pius X.* Chicago: Franciscan Herald Press, 1959.

Johnson, Paul. *Pope John Paul II and the Catholic Restoration.* New York: St. Martin's Press, 1982.

Kühner, Hans. *Encyclopedia of the Papacy.* New York: Philosophical Library, 1958.

Küng, Hans. *The Church—Maintained in Truth: A Theological Meditation.* New York: Seabury Press, 1980.

———. *Infallible? An Inquiry.* Garden City, N.Y.: Doubleday & Co., 1971.

Kurtz, Lester R. *The Politics of Heresy: The Modernist Crisis in Roman Catholicism.* Berkeley: University of California Press, 1986.

Leetham, Claude. *Rosmini: Priest, Philosopher and Patriot.* Baltimore: Helicon Press, 1957.

Little, Katharine. *François de Fenelon: Study of a Personality.* New York: Harper & Co., 1961.

Love, Thomas T. *John Courtney Murray: Contemporary Church-State Theory.* Garden City, N.Y.: Doubleday & Co., 1965.

Lubac, Henri de. *Teilhard de Chardin, the Man and His Meaning.* New York: New American Library, 1967.

Lukas, Mary, and Ellen Lukas. *Teilhard.* Garden City, N.Y.: Doubleday & Co., 1977.

Malinsky, Mieczyslaw. *Pope John Paul II: The Life of Karol Wojtyla.* New York: Seabury Press, 1979.

McCann, Dennis. *Christian Realism and Liberation Theology.* Maryknoll, N.Y.: Orbis Books, 1981.

McCormick, Richard A. "The Search for Truth in the Catholic Context." *America,* Nov. 8, 1986, pp. 276-281.

Murray, John Courtney. *The Problem of Religious Freedom.* Westminster, Md.: Newman Publishing Co., 1965.

———. *We Hold These Truths: Catholic Reflections on the American Proposition.* New York: Sheed & Ward, 1960.

Nigg, Walter. *The Heretics.* New York: Alfred A. Knopf, 1962.

Noonan, John T., Jr. *Contraception.* Cambridge, Mass.: Harvard University Press, 1965.

———. *The Scholastic Analysis of Usury.* Cambridge, Mass.: Harvard University Press, 1957.

Olf, Lillian B. *Their Name Is Pius: Portraits of Five Great Modern Popes.* Milwaukee: Bruce Publishing Co., 1941.

Oram, James. *The People's Pope.* San Francisco: Chronicle Books, 1979. (John Paul II)

———. *The Story of Karol Wojtyla of Poland.* San Francisco: Chronicle Books, 1979.

Pagani, G. B. *The Life of Antonio Rosmini-Serbati.* New York: E. P. Dutton & Co., 1906.

Pelotte, Donald E. *John Courtney Murray, Theologian in Conflict.* New York: Paulist Press, 1976.

Pohier, Jacques, and Dietmar Mieth (eds.). *The Ethics of Liberation— the Liberation of Ethics.* Edinburgh: T. & T. Clark Ltd., 1984.

Ratzinger, Joseph. "The Church's Teaching Authority—Faith— Morals." In *Principles of Christian Morality.* San Francisco: Ignatius Press, 1986.

——. *The Feast of Faith: Approaches to a Theology of the Liturgy.* San Francisco: Ignatius Press, 1986.

——. *Introduction to Christianity.* New York: Herder & Herder, 1970.

——. *The Open Circle: The Meaning of Christian Brotherhood.* New York: Sheed & Ward, 1966.

——. "Primacy, Episcopate and Apostolic Succession." In *The Episcopate and the Primacy.* New York: Herder & Herder, 1962.

——. *Theological Highlights of Vatican II.* New York: Paulist Press, 1966.

Ratzinger, Joseph, with Vittorio Messori. *The Ratzinger Report: An Exclusive Interview on the State of the Church.* San Francisco: Ignatius Press, 1985.

Rhodes, Anthony. *The Vatican in the Age of the Dictators, 1922-1945.* New York: Holt, Rinehart & Wilson, 1973.

Reardon, Bernard. *Liberalism and Tradition: Aspects of Catholic Thought in Nineteenth-Century France.* Cambridge University Press, 1975.

St. John-Stevas, Norman. *The Agonizing Choice: Birth Control, Religion and the Law.* Bloomington: Indiana University Press, 1971.

——. *Pope John Paul II, His Travels and Mission.* Boston: Faber & Faber, 1982.

Santillana, Giorgio de. *The Crime of Galileo.* New York: Time, Inc., 1962.

Schillebeeckx, Edward. *Celibacy.* New York: Sheed & Ward, 1968.

——. *Christ: The Experience of Jesus as Lord.* New York: Seabury Press, 1980.

——. *God Is Each Moment.* New York: Seabury Press, 1983.

——. *Interim Report on the Books* Jesus *and* Christ. New York: Crossroads Publishing Co., 1981.

Schillebeeckx, Edward. *Jesus: An Experiment in Christology.* New York: Random House, 1981.

———. *Marriage: Human Reality and Saving Mystery.* New York: Sheed & Ward, 1966.

———. *Ministry: Leadership in the Community of Jesus Christ.* New York: Crossroads Publishing Co., 1981.

———. *The Real Achievement of Vatican II.* New York: Herder & Herder, 1967.

Schroth, Raymond A. "Sex, God, Death and the Press." *The Christian Century,* Oct. 15, 1986, pp. 876-877.

Segundo, Juan Luis. *Theology and the Church: A Response to Cardinal Ratzinger and a Warning to the Whole Church.* Minneapolis: Winston Press, 1985.

Shannon, William. *The Lively Debate: Response to* Humanae Vitae. New York: Sheed & Ward, 1970.

Simons, Francis. *Infallibility and the Evidence.* Springfield, Ill.: Templegate, 1968.

Speaight, Robert. *The Life of Teilhard de Chardin.* New York: Harper & Row, 1967.

Spink, Kathryn. *John Paul II in the Service of Love.* New York: Mayflower Books, 1979.

Sugrue, Francis. *Popes in the Modern World.* New York: Thomas Y. Crowell Co., 1961.

Sullivan, Francis A. *Magisterium: Teaching Authority in the Church.* New York: Paulist Press, 1983.

Swidler, Leonard. *Küng in Conflict.* Garden City, N.Y.: Doubleday & Co., 1981.

Tabb, William K. (ed.). *Churches in Struggle: Liberation Theologians and Social Change in North America.* New York: Monthly Review Press, 1986.

Teilhard de Chardin, Pierre. *Let Me Explain.* New York: Harper, 1970.

Thomas, Gordon, and Max Morgan-Witts. *Pontiff.* New York: Doubleday & Co., 1983. (John Paul II)

Townsend, W. and L. *The Biography of His Holiness Pope Pius XI.* London: Albert E. Marriott Ltd., 1930.

Trevor, Meriol. *Prophets and Guardians: Renewal and Tradition in the Church.* London: Hollis & Carter, 1969.

Walsh, Michael. *An Illustrated History of the Popes, from St. Peter to John Paul II.* New York: St. Martin's Press, 1980.

Whale, John (Ed.). *The Man Who Leads the Church: An Assessment of Pope John Paul II.* San Francisco: Harper & Row, 1980.

White, Peter. "Richard Simon." *Jubilee,* December 1963, pp. 28-32.

Williams, George. H. *The Mind of John Paul II: Origins of His Thought and Action.* New York: Seabury Press, 1981.

Wojtyla, Karol. *Collected Poems.* New York: Random House, 1982.

———. *Love and Responsibility.* New York: Farrar, Straus & Giroux, 1981.

———. *Sources of Renewal: The Implementation of the Second Vatican Council.* San Francisco: Harper & Row, 1980.

———. *Toward a Philosophy of Praxis, an Anthology Edited by Alfred Block and George T. Czuczka.* New York: Cross Publishing Co., 1981.

Index

abortion, 17-18, 71, 201
Adam, Karl, 57
Alexander VI, 22; 45, 130-134
Americanism, 146, 193
Barth, Karl, 40
Bellarmine, Robert, 31, 169, 171
Benedict V, 120
Benedict VIII, 121
Benedict IX, 120-123
Benedict XIII, 138
Benedict XV, 151-152
Berengar, 118-120
birth control (*see* contraception)
Boff, Leonardo, 89-95
Boniface VIII, 123-127
Bossuet, Jacques, 174, 176-177
Calixtus III, 131
Calvin, John, 34
Celestine V, 123-124

celibacy, 19, 60, 64-65, 158-159, 201-202
Chalcedon, Council of, 53, 55
Charles V, 136-138
church-state separation, 146, 192-196
Clement II, 123
Clement VII, 129, 136-138
Clement XIV, 178
Communism, 13, 112, 149, 153, 154-155, 157-158, 161, 187
Congregation for the Doctrine of the Faith (Holy Office), 14-15, 35, 42-43, 45, 54-56, 77, 85, 93, 139, 152
Constantine, 31, 90, 116
contraception, 15, 18, 25-28, 33, 65-66, 68-69, 155-156, 162-163
Copernican theory, 15, 168-172
Curran, Charles E., 63-79, 200, 202
deduction, 15-17, 24, 39

divorce, 71-72, 202
euthanasia, 72-73
evolution, 158, 189-192
False Decretals, 28, 31
Fénelon, François, 175-178
Formosus, 117
Francis I, 136-137
Galileo, 167-173
Greeley, Andrew, 21, 164
Gregory I, 28
Gregory VI, 122-123
Gregory VII, 92, 123
Gregory XI, 128
Gregory XVI, 90, 141-142, 178-180, 188
Gutiérrez, Gustavo, 82-89
Guyon, Jeanne Marie, 175-177
Harnack, Adolf von, 186-187
Hasler, August, 35, 36
Hickey, James, 100-101
Holy Office (*see* Congregation for the Doctrine of the Faith)
homosexuality, 67, 99
Honorius I, 24, 31, 36
Humanae Vitae, 15, 23-28, 110, 161-164
Hunthausen, Raymond, 96-103
indefectibility, 33, 37, 200
Index of Forbidden Books, 24, 40, 139, 146, 152
induction, 16, 24, 201
infallibility, 16-17, 23-37, 73, 144-145, 178, 200

Innocent VIII, 131
Innocent X, 138
Innocent XI, 174-175
Innocent XII, 175-178
insemination, 70
in vitro fertilization, 70-71
John XII, 116-120
John XIX, 121
John XXII, 36
John XXIII, 14, 24, 159-160
John Paul II, 11-22, 37, 39, 44-45, 47, 48, 65, 68, 72, 77, 78, 79, 81, 93, 96, 106, 112-113, 151, 203
Julius II, 133-134
Küng, Hans, 23-48, 49, 53, 112, 200, 202
Laghi, Pio, 101
Lamennais, Felicité, de, 141, 178-182
Leo VIII, 119
Leo X, 134-136
Leo XII, 140
Leo XIII, 146-148, 184, 193
liberation theology, 81-96
Loisy, Alfred, 185-189
Louis XIV, 30, 174-177
magisterium, 17, 37, 73, 108
Marxism, 81-83, 92, 112, 155
masturbation, 66-67
Modernism, 28, 148-151, 187
Murray, John Courtney, 41, 192-197
Napoleon, 139, 140
Ottaviani, Alfredo, 54, 194, 196
Otto I, 118-120

INDEX

Otto III, 120
Papal States, 139-140, 142-143, 153
Paul V, 169
Paul VI, 15, 23, 25-26, 59, 68, 74, 112-113, 160-164
Philip the Fair, 126-127
Pius II, 131
Pius VII, 140
Pius VIII, 140
Pius IX, 17, 28, 36, 105, 142-146, 147, 154, 160, 182-185
Pius X, 90, 147-151, 185-189
Pius XI, 26, 92, 153-156, 189-192
Pius XII, 40, 70, 156-159, 192-196
Pohier, Jacques, 45
Quietism, 175-179
Ratzinger, Joseph, 43, 77-78, 88-89, 95, 105-113
Reformation, 28, 32, 64, 139
religious freedom, 15, 21, 196-197
Rosmini-Serbati, Antonio, 182-185
Savonarola, Girolamo, 132

Schillebeeckx, Edward, 46, 49-61, 202
Segundo, Juan Luis, 96
sex, premarital, 65, 67-68
Simon, Richard, 173-174
Stephen VII, 117
sterilization, 69-70
Syllabus of Errors, 28, 105, 146, 150
Sylvester III, 122
Teilhard de Chardin, Pierre, 12, 189-192
Theophylact, 120-121
Trent, Council of, 31, 32, 40
Urban VI, 128-130
Urban VIII, 139, 168-173
Vatican I, 24, 27-32, 36, 59, 145
Vatican II, 15, 21, 24, 27, 28, 32, 34, 59, 108-109, 160, 196-197
Vigilius, 31
Willebrands, Johannes, 56, 60
women, 46, 61, 92, 159
Wuerle, Donald, 101-102